# Family History
# in the Wars

How your ancestors served their country

William Spencer

the national archives

First published in 2007 by
The National Archives
Kew, Richmond
Surrey, TW9 4DU, UK

*www.nationalarchives.gov.uk*

The National Archives brings together the Public Record Office,
Historical Manuscripts Commission, Office of Public Sector
Information and Her Majesty's Stationery Office.

A catalogue card for this book is available from the British Library.

ISBN 978 1 903365 95 3

Typeset by Carolyn Griffiths, Cambridge, UK
Cover designed by Penny Jones and Michael Morris
Printed by MPG Books, Bodmin, Cornwall, UK

# Family History in the Wars

*For my editors – who I am sure
I drive mad at times!*

# **Contents**

# Foreword

A number of terms frequently appear throughout the text and perhaps these should be
explained first.

The listing of the records at the National
Archives can be found in two forms: on paper
lists and in an electronic version of the paper
lists on the Catalogue, which is available at
*www.nationalarchives.gov.uk*. It is possible to
search the Catalogue by keyword, and you
may find records of interest in more than just
the obvious places.

Many of the records now available at the
National Archives have recently been digitized.
These digitized records have been put on to a
particular section of the website which is
called 'DocumentsOnline'. You can search
DocumentsOnline by keyword and, for a fee
(to external users), download what you find.
The only cost you incur when downloading

digitized images while physically at the National Archives is when you wish to print an image to take away with you.

The records discussed in this guide cover the lives and in many cases the deaths of millions of individuals, Army, Royal Navy, Royal Air Force, Merchant Navy and civilian, male and female, old and young alike. In a guide such as this, it is not possible to give explanations in any depth, but what this book aims to do is to provide signposts to the most important records and, in many cases, what they may contain.

There are a number of reasons for describing the records in minimal terms. Many of them are variations on a theme, records of service for all three armed forces being similar in the type of data they capture, medal records listing the same medals but in different ways.

I always say that the records of service for the armed forces are arranged differently: the Army from the time you leave (discharge), the Royal Navy from the time you join, and the RAF by numbers! Anyone who has been in the armed services will understand this more readily than those who have not. Training to do certain military tasks, for instance rifle drill, was always done by numbers. What this means in the context of the records described here is that some records can be formulaic, while others are arranged in a unique way.

What can be found in the records described here will astound, frustrate or even overwhelm you. I have seen all sorts of people coming through the doors of the National Archives in search of information about someone who served in the armed forces between 1899 and 1953. Many have gone away happy; many have left with nothing. In many cases it is easy to obtain a lot of information very quickly and there are a number of reasons for this – luck, the way a particular service kept its records, or perhaps the researcher was looking for something very specific and knew it existed before going to Kew.

There are plenty of records that have failed to get into the book, either because their connection with war is too distant or perhaps they no longer exist. The records of service of the Auxiliary and, later, National Fire Service have unfortunately been destroyed. The records of service of the Palestine Police are split between St Anthony's College, Oxford, and the Empire and Commonwealth Museum in Bristol. Yet it is surprising what turns up when least expected. The Silver War Badge records for the Royal Navy only recently came to light when the Ministry of Defence Medal Office was set up.

Those who leave the National Archives with little or nothing should not necessarily give up. The reason they left with so little may be that the records have yet to be transferred from the Ministry of Defence. There are still some 142.5 million pieces of paper in the hands of the Ministry concerning records of service for those who served in the inter-war years and Second World War.

Finally, I would like to thank Catherine Bradley for so much and, of course, Kate, Lucy and Alice.

W.J.G.S.

# Introduction

Why do people want to know what an ancestor did in a war?

Many service personnel never talked about their experiences in the armed forces, especially if they saw operational service. In many cases it was because they had experienced something they did not want to share with their families, images and events they had tried to forget. For some it was because they thought those who had not been there would not understand.

It is these reasons that prompt people to spend many hours looking into the wartime past of their ancestors. Research is undertaken to provide answers to snippets from old stories, to confirm something found in an old diary, a newspaper cutting or an old photograph, or from something caught in passing conversation.

This book begins at the time of the South African/Second Boer War in 1899 and finishes at the end of the Korean War in 1953. Between these two dates, this guide will lead you to all of the key archival sources at the National Archives and some in the India Office Collection of the British Library, showing where information about ancestors who saw service in the armed forces or Merchant Navy may be found. It may also help to find information about those who came to the attention of the state, as either an alien or internee or as someone leaving the United Kingdom for a new home after the Second World War.

In order to approach many of the records discussed in this book, it is necessary to follow a few basic rules and to have as much information about the individual as possible. These rules can be applied to nearly all of the records mentioned in this book. They are in reality signposts or the basic items: who, what, why, where, when.

### When did they serve?

Many individuals had long military careers; many served in one period, left and then were either recalled (being a reservist) or volunteered for further service at a later date.

Dates are very important, as many of the records are arranged by date. For example, the records of service of personnel who served in the Army are mostly arranged by the date they left, and yet the Royal Navy records of service are arranged by date of entry into the service.

### Was the person an officer or rating/other rank/airman?

It is very important to know whether the individual you are researching was a commissioned officer or someone who served in the ranks, as this will dictate which records you need consult. If an individual was commissioned from the ranks, you may need to look in more places. The rank of a given individual at a given time is the most simple way of knowing his or her status. Tables of ranks can be found at the end of this book (pp. 228–30).

### Are you sure you know which service they served in?

Many officers' ranks have similar titles – for instance, you can be a Captain in the Royal Navy and the Army – yet they are not of equivalent rank. Captain RN is the same as an Army

Lieutenant Colonel. You can be a Sergeant in the Royal Marines, the Army and the Royal Air Force! Many individuals saw service in more than one of the armed forces. This is especially so during the First World War, when the Royal Flying Corps was part of the Army and the Royal Naval Air Service was part of the Royal Navy; in 1918 they were amalgamated to form the Royal Air Force.

### Do you know which ship/regiment/squadron they served in?

If you know the unit where an individual served, it will help you ascertain the service they were in and it may also help you to locate any operational records. If you are researching a soldier in the Army it will help if you have as much information about the unit as possible, beyond just the name. During both world wars there were hundreds of different battalions of infantry, for example, so the more specific you can be, the easier it is to locate an operational record. Many parts of the Army used similar terms to describe their units: for instance, an infantry regiment was made up of companies and units of the Royal Engineers could also be called companies, as could those in the Army Service Corps. Researching the operational records for a man in the 2nd Battalion Border Regiment will produce results, but looking for the operational records of a man in the Royal Engineers with no company number will in all probability lead nowhere. Specific unit information should lead to specific records.

**Did they die during their service?**

It is an unfortunate fact that in most cases it is easier to research someone who died in one of the wars than someone who survived. There are a number of published rolls of honour, online databases and casualty rolls that can be consulted in order to help you with your research. *The Times* newspaper is especially useful for looking for casualties, as you can search the paper by individuals' names, and this can be very helpful when looking for someone who died outside one of the major conflicts. If an individual died in either of the two world wars, start with *www.cwgc.org.*

## HOOD. (Po.)

|  |  |  |
|---|---|---|
| *Captain* | R. Kerr, CBE | 15 Feb 41 |
| *Commander* | W. K. R. Cross | 18 Sept 40 |
| | (N) S. J. P. Warrand (*act*) | 13 Mar 40 |
| | (*And as Squadron* (N) *Officer.*) | |
| *Lieut.-Com.* | G. L. Machin | 9 July 40 |
| | J. W. Hall (*ret*) | 25 Aug 39 |
| | J. G. P. Brownrigg | 6 Sept 38 |
| | (T) A. Pares | 20 June 39 |
| | (*And as Squadron* (T) *Officer.*) | |
| | C. D. Awdry (*emgcy*) | 1 Nov 39 |
| | (G) E. M. F. Moultrie | 20 Feb 41 |
| | G. E. M. Owens | 12 Aug 39 |
| *Lieutenant* | E. P. S. Lewis | 23 May 39 |
| | A. L. Kirkus | 4 July 39 |
| | D. C. Salter | 2 June 39 |
| *Tempy. Lieut., R.N.V.R.* | L. E. Friend | 15 Sept 40 |
| *Commander* (E) | R. T. Grogan | 5 May 39 |
| *Lieut.-Com.* (E) | J. G. M. Erskine | 10 July 39 |
| *Lieutenant* (E) | R. H. Dale | 15 Aug 40 |
| | H. G. E. Smith | 1 Nov 40 |
| | B. C. J. Roach (*act*) | 1 Jan 41 |
| | M. S. T. Humphrey (*act*) | 1 May 41 |
| *Tempy. Lieut.* (E) | T. F. Spence | 27 Jan 41 |
| *Major, R.M* | H. Lumley | 1 June 39 |
| *Captain, R.M.* | T. D. Cartwright | 19 Aug 40 |
| *Lieutenant, R.M.* | D. S. R. Harris | 24 Oct 40 |
| | H. D. Davies (*proby*) | 24 Aug 40 |
| *Instr. Com.* | (*Met*)(I *Fr*) D. M. Steel, MA | 6 Aug 39 |
| *Chaplain* | Rev. R. J. P. Stewart, MA | 27 Feb 41 |
| *Surg. Com.* | H. Hurst, LRCP&S | 16 Aug 40 |
| *Paym. Com.* | D. C. Roe | 25 Mar 39 |
| *Paym. Lieut.-Com. R.N.V.R.* | G. V. Carlin | 10 Oct 40 |
| *Surg. Lieut.* | J. O. Fielding, MRCS, LRCP | 2 Aug 39 |
| *Surg. Lieut., R.N.V.R.* | C. H. C. Dent, MB, BCH | 26 Aug 39 |
| *Surg. Lieut.* (D) | J. E. C. Peacock, LDS | 7 Nov 40 |
| *Paym. Lieut.-Com.* | G. V. Carlin | 10 Oct 40 |
| *Paym. Lieut.* | R. G. Phillips | 28 Jan 39 |
| *Tempy. Paym.* | | |

## Do you have any photographs of the individual in uniform?

Photographs can in many cases yield lots of useful information about someone who served in the armed forces, from the type and style of uniform to badges of rank/trade, unit badges or medal ribbons. In most cases these can be identified and dated by using a number of published sources or by asking the right person or institution. It might seem obvious, but look on the back of a photograph if you can as some thing on the back may lead your research in the right direction from the very beginning.

## Do you have any medals they earned?

Medals can be very useful tools to aid your research because in most cases they are named to the individual who earned them. If you can identify the medal, it will give you an idea of the period of service when the medal was earned. The first place to look is the *Medal Yearbook* (published annually by Token Publishing) to identify the medal. If it was an award for gallantry or meritorious service, it will be announced in *The London Gazette*, *www.gazettes-online.co.uk*. If you research an award for gallantry or meritorious conduct first, the results should lead you to much more.

### Do you have any papers/certificates relating to them?

Over a military career, service personnel are given plenty of pieces of paper to sign or keep. When an officer is commissioned, he or she is given a commission scroll. If an individual was appointed to one of the Orders of Chivalry, he should have been given a warrant appointing him to the Order. Any of these items may help you with your research and it is useful to read them very carefully looking for names, units, places and dates, all of which are useful.

## OPERATIONS GAZETTEER

The British armed forces fought in many countries throughout the world over the period 1899–1953 covered by this book, and it is important to identify the theatre of operation when researching an ancestor. Background knowledge of the military actions in which they engaged helps to determine the range of records that you may wish to explore and in which an ancestor may appear. The following is a list of the operations and wars that are mentioned in the book.

## Abor 1911–12

A punitive mission in northeast India against the Abor tribe after they had killed a mission led by an Indian Civil Service official. No British army units took part but Europeans from the Indian Army were involved. The expedition, which, also undertook survey work of the region, ran from 6 October 1911 to 20 April 1912.

## Ashanti Rising 1900

The Ashanti people rose up when it was discovered that the Golden Stool, seen as the heart of the Ashanti people, was to be seized to avoid it being used as a rallying point against British rule. Kumassi was besieged, with the Governor, Sir Frederic Hodgson, and his wife among those trapped there. Although two groups of soldiers were able to break through to Kumassi, a relief operation under Sir James Wilcox did not reach the city until 15 July, with a final relieving force arriving on 5 August.

Although very few British troops were involved in the campaign, a number of officers and specialists serving with the West African Frontier Force and other local units did take part. The Ashanti Rising took place between 31 March and 25 December 1900.

**Second Boer/South African War**

This was fought between the British Army and the two Boer independent republics of the Orange Free State and the South African Republic (Transvaal Republic) from 11 October 1899 to 31 May 1902. The political history behind the war is complex; suffice it to say that the discovery of gold in Transvaal in 1886 and access to the gold mines, the way the gold was extracted and the influx of foreigners all led to tension between those who lived in the region, the British in their colony in the Cape, the British government in London and leaders of the two Boer republics. The British moved forces up to the borders between Cape Colony and the two Boer republics. After negotiations failed to resolve the situation, war was declared on 11 October 1899 and the Boers invaded Cape Colony between then and January 1900.

Included in the numerous battles and other

minor actions during the war were the sieges of three towns, Mafeking, Ladysmith and Kimberley. In December 1899 the British suffered a number of setbacks, to such an extent that the week of 10–15 December 1899 became known as 'Black Week' after failures at Stormberg, Magersfontein and Colenso.

The war was fought in three phases: the Boer offensive between October and December 1899; the British offensives between January and September 1900; and the guerrilla phase between September 1900 and May 1902. Over 170,000 men and women saw service in the British and associated forces during the war. Some 22,000 British soldiers died during the war but only about 7,800 were battle casualties. Australia, New Zealand and Canada all sent contingents to the war. Apart from the Regular Army, many men saw service in the Imperial Yeomanry and units raised in South Africa (South African Local Forces) such as the Frontier Light Horse, Scottish Horse and Younghusband's Horse.

Nearly every regiment of the British Army took some part in the operations in South Africa between 1899 and 1902, and in many cases more than one battalion of a large number of infantry regiments took part in the war.

### The Third China War (Boxer Rebellion) 1900

An organization known as the Society of Righteous and Harmonious Fists attempted to eradicate and expel all foreigners and Christians from China. Violence increased and the foreign community in Peking was threatened. As the Chinese government were reluctant to intervene, forces from a number of European powers under the command of Admiral Edward Seymour RN landed on 10 June.

Forces from Great Britain, America, Germany and Italy all took part in operations in China. From the British perspective, the defence of the legation in Peking and its subsequent relief, and operations at Taku Forts involved sailors and marines from ships based on the China station. Soldiers from the British and Indian armies also took part in the key period of the war that ran from 10 June to 31 December 1900. Minor operations continued until September 1901.

## Burma 1930–32

Rebellion and civil unrest in Burma led to British and Indian Army forces being deployed to restore order between December 1930 and March 1932.

## Operations in India and Afghanistan 1919–39

After the First World War the British and Indian armies returned to their pre-war peacekeeping and local policing duties, which many felt was proper soldiering. Large numbers of troops were involved in the Third Afghan War in 1919, and operations in Waziristan between 1919 and 1925 and again in 1930–31 and 1935–9.

## Iraq

British and Indian Army units conducted operations in Iraq to suppress local unrest at various times between December 1919 and November 1920 and in 1928.

## Kenya

The Mau Mau War, also known as the Kenyan Emergency, started in 1952 and finished in 1960. The Mau Mau, a secret society of the Kikuyu people of Kenya, fought a terrorist war

against the British administration. A state of emergency was only declared in 1952 when British Army forces became involved in increasing numbers. A certain number of the soldiers involved in the emergency were also involved in the Korean War.

## Korea

At the end of the Second World War, Japanese troops north of the 38th parallel surrendered to the Russians while those south of it surrendered to the Americans. The 38th parallel became the border between two newly created states, the communist Democratic People's Republic in the north and the Republic of South Korea in the south!

The North Korean Army, armed by Russia and China, invaded the south on 25 June 1950. Forced back, the South Koreans were supported by the United States and the United Nations, under whose auspices other nations provided forces. A number of British forces served during the war, with the 1st Battalion Middlesex Regiment and the 1st Battalion the Argyll and Sutherland Highlanders being the first infantry to arrive in August 1950.

Perhaps one of the most well-known battles in which the British Army took part was the battle of the Imjin River in April 1951, where a large number of the 1st Battalion Gloucestershire Regiment were captured. Many of these prisoners of war endured harsh months in the hands of the Chinese and North Koreans.

The Korean War ended on 27 July 1953 when an armistice was signed.

## Malaya

The Malayan Emergency took place between 1948 and 1960 when the Malayan Races Liberation Army, a communist organization, attempted to destroy the federation agreement between the British and local Malay, Chinese and Indian leaders. The Emergency took the form of a terrorist-style war, and by its end some 2,384 British and Indian Army and local Malayan forces personnel had been killed.

## North West Frontier 1908

The British and Indian armies spent a large part of their time suppressing unruly tribes and policing civil unrest in various parts of India on numerous occasions between 1849 and 1939.

In 1908, at least two field forces were put together to deal with problems on the North West Frontier. The Bazar Valley Field Force conducted operations between 14 February and 1 March 1908, and the Mohmand Field Force between 12 and 31 May of the same year.

British Army units involved in operations on the North West Frontier in 1908 included the Northumberland Fusiliers, the Royal Warwickshire Regiment, the West Yorkshire Regiment, the Seaforth Highlanders and the Royal Munster Fusiliers

### Palestine 1936–9 and Palestine 1945–8

Opposition to British rule in Palestine before and especially after the Second World War led to internal unrest between the Palestinians and Jewish settlers, with controls over arms smuggling and the post-war influx of refugees from Europe being prime causes for the unrest. Apart from attacks on the British, there was also fighting between those living in Palestine and those arriving to settle there.

There was a break during the Second World War, but otherwise the unrest was almost constant; eventually the British forces left in June 1948, upon the creation of the state of Israel.

## Persian Gulf 1909–15

In order to suppress both the arms trade and the slave trade between various peoples based around the Persian Gulf, the Royal Navy mounted patrols to intercept ships carrying arms and slaves.

## Somaliland

At various times between 1901 and 1920, the British Army, the Royal Navy, the Royal Air Force and local African units such as the King's African Rifles were employed in trying to stop Haji Muhammad-bin-Abdullah (known to the British as the 'Mad Mullah') from continuing with the slave trade in Somaliland, and from prosecuting a religious war in the region and attacking other tribes opposed to him.

Although the majority of the forces employed in early campaigns were either soldiers or sailors, the Mad Mullah was finally defeated by aircraft of Z Force, Royal Air Force, in a short campaign between 21 January and 12 February 1920.

## Tibet 1903–4

A trade mission under the control of Colonel Sir Francis Younghusband was sent to Tibet in July 1903 but it received a hostile reception. The Tibetan Army suggested that the trade mission should return to India, but Younghusband refused to do so, launching a punitive operation against those who opposed the mission. The only complete British Army unit to take part in the operations in Tibet was the 1st Battalion Royal Fusiliers. Miscellaneous men from a variety of other British and Indian Army units also took part in the operations from 13 December 1903 to 23 September 1904.

## The First World War

The First World War was fought between 4 August 1914 and 11 November, when the armistice with Germany was signed. It is an interesting fact that the first shot of the war was fired in West Africa and the last in East Africa, yet people remember the war as being fought almost exclusively in France and Belgium on the Western Front.

The British Army fought not only in France and Belgium but also in Italy, Gallipoli, Egypt, Palestine and even China. Ships of the Royal Navy fought in most seas and oceans of the world. Rather than list all the operational theatres in which the British forces fought, the following are some of the most significant:

| | |
|---|---|
| Mons | 23 August 1914 |
| Le Cateau | 26 August 1914 |
| Marne | 6–11 September 1914 |
| Aisne | 13–25 September 1914 |
| 1st Ypres | 19 October–11 November 1914 |
| Coronel | 1 November 1914 |
| Falklands | 8 December 1914 |
| Neuve Chappelle | 10 March 1915 |
| 2nd Ypres | 22 April–25 May 1915 |
| Gallipoli | 25 April 1915–8 January 1916 |
| Loos | 25 September 1915 |
| Jutland | 31 May/1 June 1916 |
| Somme | 1 July–18 November 1918 |
| Arras | 9 April–17 May 1917 |
| 3rd Ypres | 31 July–10 November 1917 |
| German Spring Offensive | 31 March–15 July 1918 |
| Amiens | 8 August 1918 |
| Hindenburg Line broken | 29 September 1918 |
| Armistice | 11 November 1918 |

## The Second World War

Perhaps a more just war that the First World War, after only 21 years' peace the Second World War began on 3 September 1939 and went on until operations formally ended on 2 September 1945. Due to the changing nature of warfare, the aeroplane became a very important tool in prosecuting the war, especially for the British when they stood alone against Germany and Italy. This aspect of the air war is perhaps best illustrated by the fact that the Distinguished Flying Cross was the most frequently granted award for gallantry during the war.

Unlike the First World War, where civilian casualties were relatively low, in the Second World War millions of men, women and children became victims of the war, either by being killed or when they became evacuees, aliens, refugees or displaced people.

As with the First World War, so the Second World War was conducted over a large part of the globe. The following are just a few of the significant dates:

| | |
|---|---|
| 1 September 1939 | Germany invades Poland |
| 3 September 1939 | Britain declares war on Germany |

| | |
|---|---|
| 13 December 1939 | Battle of the River Plate |
| 9 April 1940 | Germany invades Norway |
| 10 May 1940 | Germany invades Belgium, Holland and France |
| 26 May 1940 | Dunkirk evacuation begins |
| 4 June 1940 | Dunkirk evacuation ends |
| 10 June 1940 | Italy declares war on Britain |
| 10 July 1940 | Battle of Britain begins |
| 31 October 1940 | Battle of Britain ends |
| 24 May 1941 | HMS *Hood* sunk |
| 27 May 1941 | *Bismarck* is sunk |
| 22 June 1941 | Germany invades Russia |
| 7 December 1941 | Japan attacks Pearl Harbor |
| 25 December 1941 | Hong Kong surrenders to the Japanese |
| 15 May 1942 | Singapore surrenders to the Japanese |
| 19 August 1942 | Dieppe raid |
| 23 October 1942 | Battle of El Alamein begins |
| 8 November 1942 | Operation Torch, the invasion of North Africa |
| 2 February 1943 | Last German troops surrender in Stalingrad |
| 16/17 May 1943 | Dambusters raid |
| 5–12 July 1943 | Battle of Kursk |
| 10 July 1943 | Operation Husky, the invasion of Sicily |
| 8 September 1943 | Italy surrenders |
| 9 September 1943 | Allies invade Italian mainland |
| 26 December 1943 | *Scharnhorst* sunk |
| 8 March 1944 | Battle for Imphal begins |
| 6 June 1944 | Operation Overlord (D Day) begins |

| | |
|---|---|
| 13 June 1944 | First V1 lands in Britain |
| 25 August 1944 | Paris liberated |
| 17 September 1944 | Operation Market Garden (Arnhem) begins |
| 22–26 October 1944 | Battle of Leyte Gulf |
| 16 December 1944 | German offensive in the Ardennes begins |
| 23 January 1945 | Troops of the 14th Army cross the Irrawaddy |
| 4–11 February 1945 | Yalta Conference |
| 19 February 1945 | US Marines land on Iwo Jima |
| 27 March 1945 | Last V2 lands on London |
| 1 April 1945 | US forces invade Okinawa |
| 7 May 1945 | Germany surrenders |
| 6 August 1945 | First atomic bomb is dropped on Hiroshima |
| 8 August 1945 | Second atomic bomb dropped on Nagasaki |
| 14 August 1945 | Japan surrenders |
| 2 September 1945 | Japanese surrender is signed on USS *Missouri* |

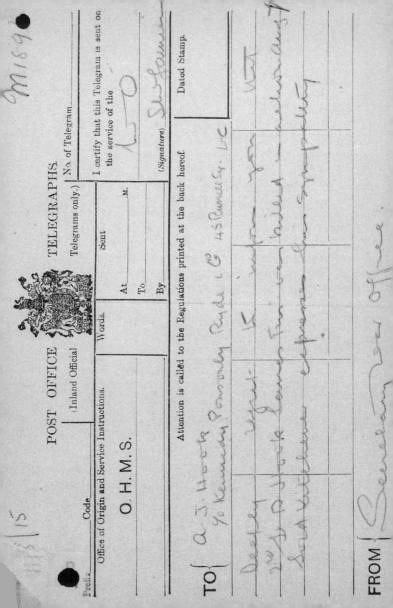

M189

11/5/15

Prefix    Code
POST OFFICE — Inland Official
O.H.M.S.
Office of Origin and Service Instructions.

TELEGRAPHS
(Telegrams only.)

No. of Telegram

Words.        Sent

At _____ M.
To _____
By _____

I certify that this Telegram is sent on the service of the

(Signature) _____

Dated Stamp.

Attention is called to the Regulations printed at the back hereof.

TO { A. J. Hook
%o Kennedy Ponsonby Ryde & Co 45 Russell Sq. LC

Deeply regret to inform you
2nd Lt D J Hook has been killed in action and
send letter express our sympathy

FROM { Secretary War Office.

# Chapter 1

# From 1899 to the end of the First World War

- The Army
  *Records of service*
  *Operational records*
  *Medals and awards*
  *Prisoners of war*
  *Courts martial*
  *Casualties*
- The Royal Navy and Royal Marines
  *Records of service*
  *Operational records*
  *Medals and awards*
- The Royal Air Force
  *Records of service*
  *Operational records*
  *Medals*
- The Merchant Navy
  *Records of service*
  *Operational records*

## SETTING THE SCENE

During the period 1899–1918, the British armed forces fought against the Boers in South Africa, suppressed risings in various parts of Africa and India, and most importantly fought against Germany and its allies in the First World War. The services grew dramatically in size during this period, and by November 1918 the weapons they were using included aeroplanes, submarines and tanks.

There are literally millions of people covered by the records for this period. Over 6 million men and women served in the Army during the period and over 6 million British war medals were issued for service in the First World War.

Between 1899 and 1918, the British armed forces were involved in numerous wars, battles and other military operations. Some of these are listed below:

2nd Boer/
South African War        11 October 1899–31 May 1902
Ashanti Rising           31 March–25 December 1900
Third China (Boxer) War  10 June–31 December 1900
Operations in
Somaliland               1901, 1902–4, 1908–10

| | |
|---|---|
| Tibet | 1903–4 |
| North West Frontier | 1908 |
| Abor | 1911–12 |
| Operations in the Persian Gulf | 1909–14 |
| First World War | 4 August 1914–11 November 1918 |

Many individuals who saw service during the period 1899–1918 could have taken part in one or more of these wars or operations, and consequently it may be possible to find records mentioning them and their activities in a number of different places.

Many researchers settle for the maximum amount of information for the minimum amount of effort (usually just the record of service if it is extant), and yet by looking for the whole picture it is possible to find out so much more. By using the operational and medal records (where applicable), it may be possible to find out what happened on a day-to-day basis, especially during the First World War.

## THE ARMY

Between 1899 and 1918 there are over 10 different records series where records of service can be found, more than five series where information about operations can be found and over 10 concerning orders, decorations and medals. While the number of different records series may appear daunting, they can all be approached without fear if the basic rules mentioned in the general introduction are followed.

The South African/Second Boer War is interesting with regard to both the Army and the records of service at that time. It was a period when not only were large numbers of reservists recalled to the colours, but new units were created specifically for service in the Boer War; and the terms and conditions of service for some units were different from those of the Regular Army. After its experiences in South Africa, numerous changes were made in the Army, perhaps the most significant being the creation of the Territorial Force (later the Territorial Army) as a result of the Territorial and Reserve Forces Act of 1907.

During the First World War there were other changes, from voluntary enlistment at the outbreak of the war to conscription from 1916. Military aviation also became very important, so much so that a new service – the Royal Air Force – was eventually created. Millions of men and women served in the First World War and over 250,000 men were commissioned as officers.

Depending upon date and type, the records are arranged differently. The records of service are arranged in one way up to 1913 and from 1914 to 1920 in another. The operational records prior to 1914 are relatively few and they are not so easy to locate. Yet between 1914 and 1918 the operational records are vast in number, far easier to identify and much easier to consult. The campaign medal records prior to the First World War are arranged by medal type and unit but with few name indexes, but for the First World War they are arranged by unit, status (officer or other rank) and medal type, and there is a name index! All of this information needs to be taken into account in order to use the records effectively.

**Records of service**

There are thousands of boxes of original records and reels of microfilm containing the records of service of men and women who saw service in the British Army or under its control between 1899 and 1918. These records, where they survive, are full of information about the people they document. However, in a large number of cases nothing survives. There are several reasons for this, the most significant being the destruction in 1940 of a large number of records of service of officers and men who saw service in the First World War. Another reason a record of service may not be found is that the individual also saw service after the First World War and their record is still held by the Ministry of Defence.

The amount and type of information found in any given record of service can vary. Most records have basic biographical information, such as when and where an individual was born, when they joined the Army, which unit(s) they served in and when they left. A record of service of an ordinary soldier is more likely to have information about his sickness record and his disciplinary record.

The biggest problem concerning the amount of information provided by any given record of service is the way records were kept by the War Office prior to 1922 and what happened to a large number of records in 1940. The record of an army officer was originally made up of three parts; the single-sheet record of service (the AF B199), yearly confidential reports (AF B196) and a correspondence file. After 1901 this was the standard way the career of an officer was recorded. The records of all officers who left the Army between 1901 and 1921, and who were not re-employed in the Second World War, went through a process whereby the AF B199 and AF B196 were selected for preservation and the correspondence file was weeded of all 'unimportant' material.

The records of all soldiers who saw service during the First World War period and who were discharged between 1914 and 1920 were processed by the Army and then stored in their record repository in Arnside Street in Bermondsey, London. Although evidence is not conclusive, it appears that soldiers' papers were in regimental corps collections and then in alphabetical order; the reason for keeping them in alphabetical order was probably the regimental number system in use up to the end of July 1920, where numbers could be duplicated, even in the same regiment or corps.

Some six million records of service were awaiting eventual transfer to the Public Record Office, together with the AF B199s and AF B196s of over 200,000 officers from the same period. On 7 and 8 September 1940, the first major air raid on London took place and one of the many buildings destroyed was the War Office record repository in Arnside Street. The majority of records awaiting transfer to the Public Record Office were destroyed, but some 10 million soldiers' records were salvaged from the debris. By 1943 the surviving records had been put into one alphabetical sequence and they were eventually transferred to the Public Record Office on microfilm as WO 363 (the 'Burnt Records'). All of the officer material selected for preservation was destroyed, but the weeded correspondence files were eventually transferred as WO 339 and WO 374. More about these can found on pp. 52–4.

So what does survive and how is it arranged? The best way to approach records of service for the period 1899–1918 is to split them up into batches by status (officer or other rank) and then by date. Added to this must be the special records relating to service in the South African/Second Boer War 1899–1902.

*Soldiers' records (Regular Army) 1899–1913*
The records of service of men who served in the British Army between 1899 and 1913 are arranged by the date the individual left the Army and not by the date he joined. Soldiers' papers for men discharged between 1883 and 1913 are arranged in two chronological periods, 1883–1900 and 1900–13, and are in the series WO 97. Both chronological ranges are arranged in alphabetical order by name. Although it helps to have as much information about an individual as possible to make sure you have the correct man, as the records are arranged in alphabetical order it is easy to identify which box you need to look in to start with.

In WO 97 there are also two supplementary series, covering discharges in 1843–99 and 1900–13. These supplementary series are also arranged by name, and in many cases the papers are for men who joined under a false name and declared their true identity at some time during their service.

**WO 97**

Although the series WO 97 is most frequently called the 'Chelsea Papers' or 'Soldier's Pension Documents', the series is in fact much more complicated. It is split into five distinct discharge periods: 1760–1854, 1855–72, 1873–82, 1883–1900 and 1900–13. There are also two supplementary sub-series of 1843–99 and 1900–13.

The key fact (relevant to this book) about WO 97 from around 1895 onwards is that it doesn't just contain the records of army pensioners, it also contains the records of men who completed a specified period of engagement in the Army which was not a pensionable term. The records of some men who died in service after 1899 may also be found in WO 97; this because widows' pensions came into being at the time of the Boer War (1899–1902).

The two supplementary sub-series 1843–99 and 1900–13 contain many records for men who joined under a false name and who only declared their true identity a number of years after enlistment.

The type of information found in the papers in WO 97 can vary slightly but in most cases you should find: the date and place of birth of the soldier; date of attestation (joining); civilian trade on enlistment; physical description; the regiment or corps he served in and his number; a medical history sheet; a conduct sheet; details of any medals earned; service overseas; if, to whom and when married; details of children; promotions; qualifications; date of discharge; and intended place of residence. If an individual moved from one regiment to another, that may also be recorded.

Most of the papers found in WO 97 are for men of the Regular Army but in some cases you can also find papers of men who had served in the Militia and who transferred into the Regular Army; you may also find papers of men who saw service in the Imperial Yeomanry and who then joined the Regular Army to see further service in South Africa between 1900 and 1903. For more information about the Militia papers and the records of the Imperial Yeomanry, see pp. 39 and 41.

The records of the Household Cavalry can be found in the series WO 400 and they are arranged by regiment and discharge period, as follows:

1 Life Guards

Series 1 1801–56
Series 2 1859–1920 *

2 Life Guards

Series 1 1799–1856
Series 2 1856–1919 *

MADROÑAS,
COBBLE HILL,
VANCOUVER ISLAND, B.C.
CANADA.

30ᵗʰ August 1915

Sir

I have the honour to acknowledge receipt
of your telegram, dated 11ᵗʰ August, informing
me that 2ⁿᵈ Lieut. D. Hook, Lancashire
Fusiliers, was killed in action on the 7ᵗʰ of
the same month.

The telegram has been forwarded to me by
my agents in England, Messrs Kennedy, Ross,
Ryde & Co., to whose care it was addressed.
They cabled the contents of the telegram to me
immediately, and doubtless they acknowledged
receipt of it, on my behalf, at the same time

I wish to say in conclusion that I well
appreciate the sympathy which Lord Kitchener
is kind enough to express.

I am, Sir
Your obedient servant
Allan J. Hook

To The Secretary
H. M. War Office
London

| Royal Horse Guards | Series 1 1805–56 |
| | Series 2 1856–86 |
| | Series 3 1886–1919 * |
| | |
| Household Battalion | Series 1 1916–19 * |

In the chronological context of this book, only those marked * are appropriate.

A small collection of papers for soldiers discharged on account of sickness, wounds or disability prior to the First World War can be found in the series PIN 71. This series is listed by name but does not include the regiment or corps in the description. The date range of each file usually represents the date of enlistment in the Army and the date when the pension ceased being paid. There are also a small number of files for widows of deceased soldiers in this series.

The papers in PIN 71 are identical to those found in WO 97 but they contain further information about the health of the subject individual, details about post-discharge medical boards and in many cases a death certificate of the individual.

*Officers' papers 1899–1913*

The majority of surviving records of service of officers commissioned into the British Army prior to 1901 are in the series WO 76. The records in this series are arranged by regiment. Depending upon the date, the description of each piece of WO 76 may have the pre-1881 numerical identity of a regiment as well as its post-1881 regimental name. Most individual volumes have an integral name index. Each volume is usually arranged according to rank, but as they are normally internally indexed knowing an officer's rank at a given time is not so important.

There are a number of problems regarding WO 76, most importantly that not all regiments and corps are represented within it and many of the records finish prior to 1913.

The records in WO 76 are available on microfilm and the information they usually contain includes: basic biographical information; date of commission and promotion(s); overseas service; medals earned; and if, to whom and when married.

Other officers' records of service can be found in WO 25, most significantly those of the Royal Engineers and some nurses who would have seen service in the Boer War. The Royal Engineer officers' records are arranged by first commission date. There is a published index of Royal Engineer officers in the library, which will provide commission dates, as would the *Army List*.

If you are researching a medical officer and you have not found any papers, you are advised to look at *Commissioned Officers* in the *Medical Service of the British Army, 1660-1960* by Alfred Peterkin (Wellcome, 1968). Another particularly useful source for medical officers is the *Medical Register*, especially the 1911 edition as it has very good potted biographies of the subject individuals.

If you are researching an army chaplain, you may find some information in *Crockford's Clerical Directory*.

In reality the best places to look for officers' papers after 1901 are in WO 339 and WO 374; see pp. 52–4.

*Militia papers*
The records of service of other ranks of the Militia are in the series WO 96, but unlike their

---

**Hart's Army List**

Hart's **Army List** was produced in our period but only up to 1915. When originally started it was set up as an alternative to the Army List with the specific aim of providing more information about an officer. For our period there is very little difference between the two, but an individual entry in Hart's will show you on a single page the career progression of an officer and tell you how many years he had been serving.

---

Regular Army equivalent in WO 97 they are arranged by unit and then by name. Most of the records in this series contain similar information to those in WO 97, but most of the records stop in about 1906, just prior to the creation of the Territorial Force (later the Territorial Army) in 1908.

The regiments found in WO 96 are arranged in regimental order of precedence. After the records of the infantry regiments come the records of the Royal Garrison Artillery Militia, whose records are arranged by country, county and then by name. Among this particular collection can be found the records for most counties of England, Scotland, Ireland and Wales.

At the end of WO 96 are the papers of soldiers discharged from the Royal Monmouthshire Royal Engineers and the Royal Garrison Regiment. The Royal Garrison Regiment was formed to garrison various parts of the empire in order to release Regular Army troops for operational service. These papers are also arranged in alphabetical order and they contain the records of a large number of men who had seen prior service in the Regular Army.

The records of officers of the Militia can be found in the series WO 68 and, as with WO 76, the records and units within the series are not complete. Once again, the information content is similar to WO 76.

The papers of officers of the Royal Garrison Regiment can be found in WO 19 and are arranged by battalion. If you do not know the battalion, try the *Army List*.

A full list of records in WO 68, arranged in alphabetical order by unit name, can be found in *Records of the Militia and Volunteer Forces 1757–1945* by William Spencer (PRO, 1997).

*Imperial Yeomanry*
The records of service of Imperial Yeomanry

other ranks are in the series WO 128 and are arranged by service number. You can find the service number in the nominal rolls of the Imperial Yeomanry, found in WO 129, but a much quicker way is to use *The Roll of the Imperial Yeomanry, Scottish Horse and Lovats Scouts: 2nd Boer War, 1899–1902* by Kevin Asplin, copies of which are in the library and Research Enquiries Room of the National Archives.

The Imperial Yeomanry attestation forms are very similar to those of the Regular Army, and the information contained within them is identical. The most obvious indication that the individual served for a short period can be found on the front of the attestation papers where they were headed 'Short service, one year's service with the colours'.

If, when looking for a set of papers in WO 128, you find a single sheet of paper with a man's name and number on it together with a five- or six-digit alpha-numeric reference, this is a good indication that after the man completed his service in the Imperial Yeomanry he joined the Regular Army for additional service. In such cases the records may be in WO 97 for discharges between 1900 and 1913. Many of the Imperial Yeomanry records found in WO 97 are for men who were medically discharged.

Apart from a very small amount of information in WO 129/12, there are no records of service for officers of the Imperial Yeomanry. It is necessary to use the *Army List* to obtain further information. Some officers of the Imperial Yeomanry were transferred or seconded from other units, so you may find using the name index in any *Army List* an effective way of finding an individual officer.

A small collection of papers concerning the Imperial Yeomanry and the commissioning of Imperial Yeomanry officers can be found in WO 108/194–223 and WO 108/397.

*South African Local Forces (1899–1902)*
The enrolment forms of men who joined for service in South Africa in such units as Bethune's Mounted Infantry, the Commander in Chief's Bodyguard and the Imperial Light Horse can be found in WO 126, with the nominal rolls of all units found in WO 126 in WO 127. The records in WO 126 provide basic biographical information and dates of service,

and the other information they capture is very similar to the records found in WO 97.

A full list of the South African Local Forces and their associated records, the nominal rolls, enrolment forms and medal rolls for the Queen's and King's South Africa Medals, can be found in the paper copy of the WO 100 catalogue.

A number of the South African forces changed their names during the war and consequently you may need to look for papers under the new unit name as well as the old one.

*British Army other ranks' papers 1914–20*
Although the arrangement of the surviving records of service for men discharged from the British Army between 1 January 1914 and 31 December 1920 may be easily explained, that is where simplicity ends.

The two most important collections of papers are to be found in WO 363 (known as the 'Burnt Papers') and WO 364 (frequently called the 'Unburnt Papers'). WO 363 are the papers that were salvaged from the Arnside Street fire in 1940 and they were placed in alphabetical order before the end of the Second World War. WO 364 are the records returned to the War Office by other government departments, most notably the Ministry of Pensions, after the Arnside Street fire, to supplement the surviving records still in the hands of the War Office. Both series are arranged in a form of alphabetical order, which may sound simple, but when there are over 50 reels of microfilm covering the name John Smith you need a little more to find your man.

WO 364 is arranged in three distinct A–Z sequences. Within a numerical range of films for a common name, you should, if necessary, be able to work your way through one reel of microfilm after another in order to locate the correct individual.

The arrangement of WO 363 is slightly more problematic. Each letter of the alphabet has its own index, arranged in ranges of names. Therefore you may find that, for example, James Dunn is on WO 363 D 1086 and WO 363 D 1144. If this is the case it may not be possible to go from reel to reel in a consecutive numerical sequence of films, as it may be necessary to jump a few reels. In order to avoid this confusion, pay particular attention to the WO 363 catalogue, so as to ensure you have the correct reel of microfilm.

The records of service of men with common names, such as John Smith, are in many cases arranged in regimental number order. While this arrangement is useful, not everyone knows the regimental number of the individual they are looking for! Another slight flaw in the arrangement of common names by regimental number is that the Army was renumbered during the war, when, for example, the men of the Territorial Force (later the Territorial Army) were given new six-digit service numbers. The records of a Territorial Force soldier may be filed by his old number or by his six-digit number and you will therefore have to look for both! The number used on the sheet at the beginning of a man's record of service may not be the only one he served under, and it may be necessary to read the record of a man very carefully in order to eliminate him from your search.

In order to use both series effectively, it helps to have as much information as possible about your soldier before you start. I call this having a 'unique identifier'. All of the following may help you locate the specific record that you require:

- name;
- rank;
- number;
- regiment/corps;
- date and place of birth;
- other information about his family, such as wife's or child's name.

What this list of helpful items of information indicates is that this is the sort of information you may find recorded on a soldier's papers apart from the routine things such as promotions, medical and disciplinary history sheets, medal details and, of course, when a man joined and left.

The two series WO 363 and WO 364 have biases in their content, and while I recommend that you search both, there are a couple of ways to prioritize your search.

It is sensible to look in WO 363 first if the soldier you are looking for:

- died in service;

- was killed in action;
- died of disease;
- died of wounds;
- was executed,

You should look in WO 364 first if the soldier you are researching:

- was discharged through sickness;
- was discharged through wounds;
- was an old soldier who was discharged on age grounds,

Of all of the forms you may find in a First World War-period record of service, the Army Form B103, 'Casualty form – active service', is probably the most informative as it will record when a soldier joined, when he was promoted, where posted, when he went to hospital, whether he was decorated and if, when and where he was killed. If you find an AF B103, it will enable you to use the other records concerning all aspects of the First World War much more effectively, because it will give you what a historian works with: names, places and dates.

**Unique identifiers**

The biggest problem when researching a member of the armed forces is to find an item of information that will set that person apart from all others, especially when looking for someone with a common name. A regimental/service/ official number is one of the most important items of information to have when looking for someone who served in the ranks. The Royal Navy was the first service to have a one man–one number system, which started on 1 January 1873. The Royal Marines started their number system in the autumn of 1884.

Army numbering was not sorted into a one man–one number system until August 1920. Prior to this, it was possible for more than one man to have the same number even when serving in the same regiment. An example of regimental numbering at its worst has to be during the First World War, where one infantry regiment could have two regular battalions, a special reserve battalion, a militia battalion, a number of territorial battalions and service battalions. In theory, it was possible for the same number to be used in each of the battalions. The Territorial Army was renumbered during the war, when each man was given a new six-digit number.

Unusual names help when carrying out research. I once had to search for a First World War soldier who transferred from the infantry to the Royal Flying Corps and then the Royal Air Force. According to his Medal Index Card, his initials were L.V.G. and his surname was St Clair. Most Medal Index Cards for other ranks give at least the first name, but not in this case. Why? Probably because his full name was Lulu Victor Gerald St Clair!

Although both series are meant to contain the records of men who were discharged from the Army between 1914 and 1920, it is possible to find many records of men who were discharged earlier and who had no connection with the First World War. On the odd occasion it is also possible to find papers for men who saw service into the late 1920s, but this is a rare exception and not the rule.

Both series WO 363 and WO 364 are being digitized and placed online at *www.ancestry.co.uk*. For those who wish to search for and download these records via the Ancestry website, you can do this for an individual fee or you can take out a subscription for all of their services. Access to the Ancestry website is free at the National Archives, where the only costs you incur are any printing costs. The great advantage of digitizing WO 363 and WO 364 is that it will be possible to do specific searches for an individual by name, number and unit.

A collection of some 22,000 files of men and women, officers and other ranks who were discharged from the forces, primarily the Army, can be found in the series PIN 26. This series can be searched by surname through the Catalogue but the descriptions do not include the regiment/corps in which the individual served. The first date in the file description usually indicates the date of enlistment and the last date gives the year of death of the soldier. The series contains some very interesting files, including one notorious murderer, John Christie, and even a soldier of the South Wales Borderers (formerly 24th Foot) who was awarded the Victoria Cross for conduct at Rorke's Drift in 1879!

*British Army officers' papers 1914–21*
Two key series cover the records of service of officers who saw service in the First World War; as might be expected, they represent different elements of the Army and they are also arranged differently.

Although it is possible to search for First World War officers' papers by name on the Catalogue, doing so does have its pitfalls, most notably that many of the file descriptions give only a single initial and do not note the regiment/corps in which the individual served.

*WO 339 Officers' Services, First World War, Long Number Papers (numerical)*

This contains the records of 139,908 officers, most of whom were commissioned into the Regular Army. The series is arranged by 'Long Number' (the original War Office reference), an index of which can be found in WO 338.

WO 338 is available on microfilm and is arranged by surname. Each entry in this series is spread across the page in the order: surname, forename and initial(s), regiment or corps, Long Number, rank.

The regiment or corps is usually abbreviated in the case of a corps or the Guards, but infantry regiments are identified by their pre-1881 numerical identity. A full list of regiments and their pre-1881 numerical identities can be found on pp. 224–7.

Once you have identified the individual and his Long Number, you can then use that in the WO 339 catalogue. Look for the Long Number down the right-hand side of the page. If you find it, move across to the left-hand side of the page, where you will find the WO 339 piece number. You can then order the WO 339 piece number on the ordering computer. It is also possible to use the Long Number to search the Catalogue by putting it in the 'go to reference' box in the top left-hand corner of the Catalogue search page.

When using WO 338, you may on occasions come across references in a format such as BO/235 or P/10505. BO/235 is what is called a 'Vowel Reference', and these files can be found in WO 374. P/10505 is what is called a 'P or Personal File', and these records are still retained by the Ministry of Defence. If you find an entry for an individual in WO 338 where the Long Number is in brackets, this usually indicates that the file has been given either a Vowel Reference or a P File. Although the recommended research technique would be to go to the series WO 374 in the case of Vowel References and the Ministry of Defence for P Files, it is always worth applying the bracketed Long Number to the WO 339 catalogue, as errors have been made where a file which is indicated in one record series is actually in another one!

WO 339/139092–906 (Long Numbers 289026–995) contains the other-rank records of a number of British Army soldiers who were commissioned into the Indian Army. These files represent only their British Army service, the remainder being held at the British Library. Among the files in WO 339 are those for the well-known war poets Siegfried Sassoon and Robert Graves.

*WO 374 Officers' Services, First World War, personal files (alphabetical)*
This contains the files of 77,829 officers, most of whom were commissioned into the Territorial Force or for specific service on the 'General List'. The file of Lawrence of Arabia can be found in WO 374.

*Officers' files: contents*
The content of most files in WO 339 and WO 374 appears to be very boring, and this is because they are the remaining third – all that is left – of an officer's file. The other two-thirds, the interesting bits, were destroyed by enemy action in 1940. What remains is primarily concerned with money, although if an officer was captured you may find his repatriation report, giving the circumstances of his capture. If an officer was commissioned from the

ranks, you will usually find his other-rank papers in his file.

The records of a few senior and selected officers, including Sir Douglas Haig and the poet Wilfred Owen, can be found in the series WO 138.

*WO 398 Women's (later Queen Mary's) Army Auxiliary Corps: Service Records*
Surviving records of service of the Queen Mary's Army Auxiliary Corps can be found in the records series WO 398. These records, much like the records in WO 363, are the remnants of the papers that survived the Arnside Street fire in 1940.

Arranged in alphabetical order, these records contain basic biographical details, enlistment information and where individuals served. If you are lucky, you may find a medical history sheet. The records have been digitized and are available on DocumentsOnline; they can be searched by name.

*Nurses*
Although there are some early nurses' records of service in WO 25, the key collection is WO

399. This series covers nurses of the Queen Alexandra's Imperial Military Nursing Service, Queen Alexandra's Imperial Military Nursing Service Reserve and the Territorial Force Nursing Service. WO 399 is arranged in two alphabetical sequences, one covering the Queen Alexandra's Imperial Military Nursing Service and the Queen Alexandra's Imperial Military Nursing Service Reserve, and the other covering the Territorial Force Nursing Service. Don't be fooled by the date description of 1914–22, as the records of many nurses who saw service prior to 1914 can be found in this series. The records of many nurses who saw service in the Boer War can be found in WO 399, which can be searched on the Catalogue by name.

Information about nurses who were decorated during the First World War can sometimes be found in *The Nursing Times*. Access to digitized copies of *The Nursing Times*, where the paper can be searched by name or subject, can be found at *www.rcnarchive.rcn.org.uk*.

*The Indian Army*
The records of service for Indian Army

personnel are held at the British Library, the majority being in the series L/MIL/14. A full alphabetical index of the files in L/MIL/14 can be found on the open shelves in the Asian and African Studies reading room at the British Library. Also available in the same room are copies of the Indian *Army List* and lists of officers commissioned into the Indian Army Reserve of Officers.

The other-ranks records of service of a number of men of the British Army who were commissioned into the Indian Army during the First World War can be found in WO 339.

It is possible to look at Indian *Army Lists* in the library at the National Archives but they only cover the period 1902–39. Certain Indian Army officers also appear in the British *Army List*.

*Conscientious objectors*
In August 1915 men and women between the ages of 16 and 65 were required to register for what became the National Register. Details provided for the register included age, sex, occupation and whether the individual was willing to work for the state. The National

Register was eventually used by the state to identify men for conscription.

Conscription was introduced after the passing of the Military Service Act 1916, and a consequence of this was that many individuals registered as conscientious objectors. During the First World War, the registration of conscientious objectors was a local responsibility.

Tribunals were set up to hear the cases of those individuals who thought they should be exempt from military service, as well as the cases of conscientious objectors. The series MH 47 consists of the records of the Middlesex Tribunal, and papers relating to exemptions and conscientious objections can be found within this series. Lists of cases can be found in MH 47/126–35 and an alphabetical card index can be found in MH 47/136–41.

## Operational records before the First World War

War diaries, giving day-to-day accounts of the activities of individual units, did not come into being until the publication of *Field Service Regulations, Part II*, of 1909. Prior to this, it was the responsibility of all field commanders to furnish their superiors with reports and despatches relating to their activities.

Information concerning operations before 1914 can be found in the series WO 33 and WO 32. The best way to search these two series is by keyword, using place of battle, country or geographical region, and using such terms as 'report', 'operation(s)' or 'despatch'.

Operational records for the Boer War can be found in WO 105 and WO 108. Records concerning operations in East or West Africa may be found in the appropriate Colonial Office (CO) series relevant to the colony. You may also find reports in CO 445 West African Frontier Force or CO 534 King's African Rifles.

Despatches for many pre-First World War operations were published in *The London Gazette*, and these can be found by searching via *www.gazettes-online.co.uk*.

Reports of many military operations were published as Parliamentary Papers and these can be located via the electronic published works link at the internal National Archives website.

The National Archives library has plenty of published works concerning military operations for all periods. Please ask at the library desk or use the library catalogue.

### Operational records in the First World War

As already stated, Unit War Diaries came into being in 1909 and the first use of such records was in the First World War. *Field Service Regulations 1909, Part II*, Chapter XVI, paragraph 140, laid down what should be kept in a war diary and for what purpose. One important use of the war diary, forgotten by many who now read them, was 'To collect information for future reference with a view to effecting improvements in the organisation, education, training, equipment and administration of the army for war.'

The Unit War Diaries for the period 1914–23 can be found in the series WO 95. These diaries provide a unique day-to-day account of the activities of nearly all the major units and organizations in the British Army in the First World War, from General Headquarters to units such as field bakeries. The series is arranged by operational theatre, i.e. France, Gallipoli, Egypt, etc., and then in a strict hierarchy: General Headquarters, army, corps, division, brigade, etc. It is possible to search the Catalogue for units by their identity. I would suggest that you try and keep things simple, so if you are looking for a Royal Garrison Artillery siege battery, just use the battery number. If you are looking for an infantry regiment, use the battalion number as well as the name. There are many ways to search for a war diary, using wildcards such as * and by combining searches using the term 'AND'.

The records in WO 95 can vary in detail. The diaries at the higher level of command do not mention individuals as frequently as those further down the chain of command. Officers are mentioned quite frequently, whereas other ranks may only be mentioned occasionally, for example when they receive an award.

If you are researching the activities of an infantry battalion, it is frequently worthwhile going up the chain of command and looking at the headquarters diary for the brigade or division to which a particular infantry battalion belonged. This is especially so when a battalion was in heavy fighting, as some information can be recorded at a higher level as well as, or in some cases instead of, at battalion level.

A basic chain of command at all levels for which war diaries can be found would look like this:

General Headquarters
Army
Corps
Division
Brigade
Infantry battalion

There are many diaries for the cavalry and many units that did not sit in this type of structure. You can find diaries for hospitals, field ambulances, labour corps units, and Australian, Canadian, New Zealand and South African forces. Diaries for units of the Indian Army, the King's African Rifles and the West African Frontier Force are also in WO 95.

It may seem strange that the records of the 63rd (Royal Naval) Division are in WO 95. After being under the operational control of the Admiralty during their land operations in Gallipoli in 1915, the Royal Naval Division was transferred to War Office control in 1916 and hence their operational records from 1916 onwards are in WO 95. The earlier Royal Naval

Division operational records can be found in ADM 137.

Many units saw service in more than one operational theatre. As a result, you may find a unit with more than one diary, each one of them representing service in a different part of the world. It is important, therefore, when searching WO 95 to note the date of the diary, as you may find the right unit but the wrong place and date.

The other key source for operational history in the First World War is the series WO 158, the Military Headquarters papers. Although they do not always mention individuals, they can tell you what units were doing. They are also good for information about the planning of battles. One of the strengths of the records in WO 158 is the wealth of information regarding operations in East Africa.

The final operational sources for the First World War are the trench and other maps in WO 153 and WO 297. There are also maps for the other operational theatres of the period, but those for the Western Front, as mentioned above, are the maps most widely used.

| WO 298 | Salonika |
| WO 300 | German South West Africa and German East Africa |
| WO 301 | Gallipoli |
| WO 302 | Mesopotamia |
| WO 303 | Palestine |
| WO 369 | Italy |

The official histories of the First World War are available in the library.

### Campaign medals before the First World War

Millions of medals were awarded to men and women of the British Army during the period 1899–1918, for service all over the globe. The greatest number of medals granted during this period were awarded for service in the First World War, but it is to Africa that we must look first.

Two campaign medals were awarded for service in the Boer War and another for service in the Mediterranean, where militia soldiers relieved regular soldiers so that they could go and fight in South Africa.

During the same period but specifically in 1900, British Army personnel were engaged in operations in a number of different places around the world, which led to them receiving campaign medals. For example:

| | |
|---|---|
| the Queen's South Africa Medal | for service in South Africa; |
| the Queen's Mediterranean Medal | for garrison service in Malta and Gibraltar; |
| the China Medal | for service in the Boxer Rebellion; |
| the Ashanti Medal | for service in West Africa. |

Campaign medals are in most cases the only tangible things between the events they represent, the recipient and now. They are great signposts for the researcher, for not only are most of them named, but they can usually provide you with lots of information about a soldier's career.

Lists of those eligible for campaign medals are called medal rolls, and those for the Army can be found in the series WO 100 for all campaigns apart from the First World War.

WO 100 is arranged according to the campaign and its associated medal. Each collection of rolls for each specific medal is then arranged in what is called the 'regimental order of precedence', whereby the regiment/corps which was founded first is at the beginning, with others following in the order in which they were founded. Each specific medal roll may then be broken down, first by battalion (if necessary) and then in alphabetical order, with the officers listed by rank and then either by seniority (when they reached that rank) or in alphabetical order. The other ranks are usually listed in alphabetical order.

The medal rolls for the Queen's South Africa Medal are particularly complicated as they can include both regular and militia battalions, volunteer service companies and odd men attached, and they may appear in a very disorganized manner.

Some medal rolls simply record entitlement to a medal, but others may record entitlement to clasps representing specific battles or places or other events. In many cases it may be necessary to look in more than one roll in order to verify entitlement to a medal with a number of clasps.

During the period 1899–1918, but not including the First World War medals, a soldier may have qualified for one or more of the following:

the East and West Africa Medal;
the India Medal 1895;
the Khedive's Sudan Medal 1896–1908;
the East and Central Africa Medal;
the Queen's South Africa Medal;
the Queen's Mediterranean Medal;
the King's South Africa Medal;
the China Medal 1900;
the Ashanti Medal;
the Africa General Service Medal;
the Tibet Medal;
the India General Service Medal 1908–35;
the Khedive's Sudan Medal 1910.

## Campaign medals in the First World War

The medal rolls for campaign medals awarded for the First World War are in the series WO 329, arranged according to medal and then by officers and other ranks. There are also rolls for a large number of civilians who qualified for medals.

The index to the rolls in WO 329 can be found in WO 372 and the series is known as the 'Medal Index Cards'. These cards are arranged in alphabetical order and regimental order of precedence. Although the cards are available on microfiche, they have also been digitized and made available on DocumentsOnline. It is therefore possible to search by any combination of name, rank, number and unit(s), which makes things much easier.

When searching for a Medal Index Card on DocumentsOnline it may be necessary to use initials rather than forename(s), especially for officers. Individuals with hyphenated surnames may be found by using the whole surname, the last half only, or the last half in full with the first letter of the first half as an initial rather than in its entirety.

Each individual index card contains the name, rank(s), number(s) and unit(s) an individual served with when qualifying for their campaign medals. Down the left-hand side is an indication of the medals he or she qualified for, together with the original Army Medal Office references for the appropriate medal roll(s). On the right-hand side of most Medal Index Cards is an area for remarks. In this area may be recorded information such as the fact that the recipient was killed, was taken prisoner of war or was commissioned. At the bottom of many index cards will be the term 'Em', 'Emb' or 'Emblems', which indicates that the individual was Mentioned in Despatches.

A frequent annotation on the cards of those

personnel who received the 1914 Star is 'Clasp and Roses' or 'C and R'. This means that the individual received the dated clasp on their 1914 Star, indicating that they saw service under fire between 5 August and 22 November 1914.

On most Medal Index Cards the following medals may be recorded:

- the 1914 Star;
- the 1914/15 Star;
- the British War Medal;
- the Victory Medal;
- the Territorial Force War Medal.

Some cards may also record:

- the Silver War Badge, usually noted as 'SWB List', with a number.

If an individual was awarded a Silver War Badge, they may have been discharged on account of sickness or wounds. If this is so it is worth converting the reference into the appropriate roll, as it will tell you when an individual enlisted, when they were discharged and why

F 1769                                              F 1769

Name in full: *Arthur Bedward Spencer*

Date of Birth *15 April 1891*
Place of Birth *Nottingham. Notts.*
Occupation *Hosier Manft r*

| Date and Period of Engagements | Age | Height Ft. In. | Chest In. | Hair | Eyes | Complexion | Wounds, Scars, or Marks |
|---|---|---|---|---|---|---|---|
| 7 Nov r. 1914. – For hostilities. F.B. | | 5  11½ | 35 | Auburn | Grey | Fresh | Vac: 3 L. |

| Ship, &c., served in | List | No. | Rating | Period of Service From | To | If Discharged, whither and for what cause | Sub-ratings. Rating | From | To | Character & Ability C | Date | A | Remarks |
|---|---|---|---|---|---|---|---|---|---|---|---|---|---|
| Pembroke III. | 1st | 1131 | F.B. Once | 5/9 Nov r 31 Oct 15 | | | | | | Vy superior | & | | R 3145/15. |
| President II | " | " | " | 10 1 1 31 Augt | | Shore Armd cars Reestanded | | | | b 9 | Sat | | Gra d his courage & Proby Slight Suff R.N.A.S s 9 E N 9 + 9 15. Appme xchange to shore |
| | | | | | | | | | | | | | |
| Armd Car &c d Service Abroad | | | | 26 Ap 15 | | D. Lg 67 President II | | | | | | | |

*See card index "Armd Car Divn France"*

FOR SERVICE IN [stamp]
LAND OPERATION
See N.P. 795/16 (1 g19)
N.P. 790/16 (S 19)

| BADGES | | |
|---|---|---|
| No. | Granted | Deprived |
| | | |

CLASS FOR CONDUCT

CLOTHING & BEDDING

– when there may be no surviving record of service, this adds just a little more.

On some cards other medals may be recorded, such as:

- the India General Service Medal 1908–35;
- the General Service Medal 1918–62;
- the Africa General Service Medal 1902–56.

The medal rolls for the medals above are in WO 100.

### Long service medals

Regular Army soldiers who served at least 18 years with good conduct throughout could be recommended by their commanding officer for the Long Service and Good Conduct Medal, and the rolls for these are in WO 102. Arranged by period and unit, these rolls are very useful for calculating when an individual joined the Army and when they were likely to be discharged to pension. The rolls for 1901–19 have been digitized and are available on DocumentsOnline. Although it is not possible to search by name, you can search by regiment/corps.

A number of other rolls for long service and good conduct awards, such as those for the Special Reserve, Militia and Imperial Yeomanry, can also be found in WO 102.

## Gallantry and meritorious service awards before the First World War

All awards for gallantry and meritorious service were announced in *The London Gazette*. It is possible to access *The London Gazette* at *www.gazettes-online.co.uk*, and it is also possible to look at it at the National Archives in the series ZJ 1.

Recommendations for awards prior to the First World War may be found in WO 32, WO 105 and WO 108, the latter two series relating specifically to the Boer War. The files in WO 32 contain recommendations for the Victoria Cross, the Distinguished Service Order and the Distinguished Conduct Medal.

Citations for the Victoria Cross can also be found in the series WO 98, which has been digitized and placed on DocumentsOnline. It is possible to search by the name of the Victoria Cross recipient.

Registers for the Distinguished Service

Order and the Distinguished Conduct Medal can be found in WO 390 and WO 391 respectively.

## Gallantry and meritorious service awards in the First World War

Recommendations for awards for gallantry or meritorious service were submitted on an Army Form W3121 but unfortunately all of those for the period 1914–18 were destroyed by enemy action in 1940. Surviving sources for information concerning awards are restricted to a number of key sources.

All awards granted for gallantry or meritorious service were announced in *The London Gazette*, and this is available online at *www.gazettes-online.co.uk*, in the series ZJ 1 or for the period 1914–20 on microfilm. The indexes for the First World War are available on the open shelves in the Microfilm Reading Room at the National Archives. Each index covers three months of the year and provides the type of award, the names of the recipients and the page on which the award was announced.

There are separate name indexes on

microfiche for the Distinguished Conduct Medal, the Military Medal, the Meritorious Service Medal and those Mentioned in Despatches. These indexes have been digitized and are searchable by name on DocumentsOnline.

The register of the Distinguished Service Order is in the series WO 390 and is arranged in gazette date order. There are name indexes in each of the volumes.

A name index for the Military Cross is available in WO 389/9–24 and all of the gazette announcements for these awards are in WO 389/1–8.

The register of the Distinguished Conduct Medal is in the series WO 391 and is arranged according to date of campaign, with each one then in gazette date order.

Many of the awards announced in *The London Gazette* were accompanied by a citation, but there were no citations for the Military Medal, Meritorious Service Medal, the Distinguished Service Order or the Military Cross when they were announced as part of a New Year or Birthday Honours List.

Published citations for winners of the

Victoria Cross can be found in WO 98, which has been digitized and can be searched by name on DocumentsOnline.

## Prisoners of war

Officers and men captured during the Boer War 1899–1902 are frequently listed in the casualty lists published in *The Times* newspaper, access to the digitized version of which is available via the public computer terminals at the National Archives. The published casualty roll also contains the list of men taken prisoner: *The Boer War Casualty Roll, 1899–1902: An Alphabetical Listing* by Alexander M. Palmer (Military Minded, 1999).

In the series WO 161 can be found a number of reports filed by individual officers and men of the British Army during and about their experiences as prisoners of war. There are not very many compared with the number of men captured by the Germans and their allies, but what is available has been digitized and made available via DocumentsOnline. It is possible to search by name and regiment/corps.

The records of the Foreign Office department responsible for prisoners of war can be found in FO 383 and these records have been catalogued to a level whereby it is possible to search by name.

A published list of officers taken prisoner between 1914 and 1918 can be found in: *List of British Officers Taken Prisoner in the Various Theatres of War between August 1914 and November 1918*, compiled from records kept by Messrs Cox and Co. (London Stamp Exchange, 1988).

### Courts martial

Army courts martial could be heard at a number of different levels according to offence and the operational conditions at the time. The most common sort of court martial was that carried out at regimental level, where the commanding officer tried those offences whose punishment was within his powers.

Courts martial at District, General or Field General level were usually for the more serious offences, and when operational circumstances were such that trials had to be conducted close to where operations were taking place.

There are many series where information

about courts martial may be found, and these include:

WO 71 Courts Martial Proceedings
   This series contains most of the papers for those
   executed in the First World War.
WO 90 District Courts Martial Abroad
WO 92 District Courts Martial Home
WO 213 Register of Courts Martial 1909–63

Most information concerning courts martial was entered into the records by the date it was received at the Judge Advocate General's Office.

## Casualties

There are a number of primary and secondary sources that can be used to find out more about men who died between 1899 and 1918. The following is a list of the key sources:

- The files WO 129/8–11 contain information on Imperial Yeomanry casualties for the Boer War.
- C. Hobson, *Airmen Died in the Great War, 1914–1918: The Roll of Honour of the British and Commonwealth Air Services of the First World War* (Hayward, 1995).
- Steve Watt, *In Memoriam: Roll of Honour Imperial Forces, Anglo-Boer War 1899–1902* (University of Natal Press, 2000).

- Alexander M. Palmer, *The Boer War Casualty Roll, 1899–1902: An Alphabetical Listing* (Military Minded, 1999).
- *Soldiers Died in the Great War 1914–19: A Complete and Searchable Database* (Naval and Military Press, 1998). This database also includes officers.
- Of all the online resources, the Commonwealth War Graves Commission website at *www.cwgc.org* provides access to the Commission's database of those buried in their cemeteries or commemorated on one of their memorials.

*Further reading*
See the following for more information.

MEDALS
William Spencer, *Medals: The Researcher's Guide* (The National Archives, 2006)

THE ARMY IN THE FIRST WORLD WAR
William Spencer, *Army Service Records of the First World War*, 4th edition (The National Archives, 2008)

## THE ROYAL NAVY AND ROYAL MARINES 1899–1918

The term 'Royal Navy and Royal Marines' in the context of service records includes the Royal Naval Reserve, the Royal Naval Volunteer Reserve, the Royal Marine Light Infantry, the Royal Marine Artillery and the Royal Naval Division. The Royal Naval Air Service can also be included under the heading of the Royal Navy, but information concerning their records can be found under the Royal Air Force. Similarly, information about the operation records of the 63rd (Royal Naval) Division may also be found under operational records of the Army.

The period 1899–1918 saw the Royal Navy operating all over the world, fighting at sea (both on it and under it), on the land and in the air. The changes in technology and the growth of the service are reflected in the records, from the specialization of naval ratings to the operational records of submarine and naval air squadrons.

Due to the complex nature of the Royal Navy in all its guises, it is very important to know which part an individual belonged to, be it the Royal Navy, the Royal Naval Reserve, the

Royal Naval Volunteer Reserve or the Royal Naval Air Service. There are usually clues that will indicate which part of the Royal Navy an individual belonged to. If you don't have these indicators, it is not the end of your research: it will just take you longer to find them as you have to eliminate all of the possibilities, one by one!

Many of the ships mentioned in a naval record of service were not floating vessels but were names given to the various shore establishments. In order to ascertain whether a name was a ship or what are sometimes called 'concrete frigates', see the following books:

- J.J. Colledge, *Ships of the Royal Navy* (Greenhill, 2003)
- Ben Warlow, *Shore Establishments of the Royal Navy* (Maritime Books, 1992).

### Records of service

Royal Navy ratings – and indeed all ratings of the Royal Navy, the Royal Naval Reserve and the Royal Naval Volunteer Reserve – always have numbers, and these are the key to finding a record of service. According to the date the individual served, the number may be just numerals, but as the Navy got bigger and more complicated, so letters as prefixes or suffixes were added in order to indicate something of importance, whether it be a specialization or trade, a length of service or a division.

A useful guide to the service numbers of the Royal Navy, the Royal Naval Reserve, the Royal Naval Volunteer Reserve and other naval forces can be found in *Naval Long Service Medals 1830–1990* by K.J. Douglas-Morris (Naval and Military Press, 1991), a copy of which can be found in the library at the National Archives.

## ADM 188 Royal Navy Ratings

The series ADM 188 contains the records of service of all Royal Navy ratings serving on 1 January 1873, when the official number system started, or who joined on 1 January 1873 or at any time up to 1923. Arranged by official number, the whole of ADM 188 has been digitized and is now available on DocumentsOnline. It is possible to search by name and/or official number.

Prior to 1908, anyone joining the Royal Navy

would be given an official number made up of numerals only. From 1908 alphabetical prefixes were added to official numbers to indicate the specialization of the rating; these were:

| | |
|---|---|
| J | Seamen |
| K | Stokers |
| L | Officers' stewards and officers' cooks |
| M | Miscellaneous |

In 1903 the Royal Navy started a system of 'short service' for the seamen and stoker branches, for those men who wanted to serve for fewer than 12 years. The prefix for the official numbers of these men was SS. Short service seamen had numbers in the range 1 to 12000 and stokers in the range 100000 to 126000. The usual term of engagement for short service enlistment was five years' full-time service and seven years in the reserve.

Ratings joining the Royal Naval Air Service from July 1914 to 31 March 1918 were given official numbers prefixed 'F'.

If you are unable to locate a record of a Royal Navy rating in ADM 188 on DocumentsOnline by searching by name or official number, there are a number of alternatives you can pursue. The name index of ADM 188 is available on microfilm, so you could search that first, get the official number and then go back to DocumentsOnline. If you have any medals, look at them around the edge or on the back, as they should be named with the details you need to use ADM 188.

*ADM 196 Royal Navy Officers*
The records of service of most Royal Navy officers are preserved in the series ADM 196 but the series is not the easiest to use.

Many of the records in ADM 196 are arranged by specialization and by seniority, both of which can be ascertained by using the *Navy List*. The specialization of a naval officer indicated his particular training and role, such as executive officers who could command a ship and civil officers, including surgeons and paymasters. The seniority of an officer is the date of appointment at a given rank.

The records in ADM 196 take the form of statements of service, listing ships on which served, promotions and various remarks.

Some of the records are in the form of Confidential Reports.

There are a number of indexes associated with ADM 196, either card indexes or index volumes. The index volumes are usually arranged in alphabetical order and the references are to a volume and age number. The volume number needs to be converted into an ADM 196 reference. The card indexes associated with ADM 196 are arranged in name order and provide you with complete ADM 196 references (volume and page) and the original source from which the information was extracted. The index cards do not need to be converted.

The biggest problem with ADM 196 is that not all of the records of service for some particular specializations have survived. A number of volumes for engineers and Warrant Officers are in fact missing despite being mentioned in some of the records or indexes.

### ADM 104 Naval Surgeons
Although there are a number of volumes of ADM 196 that hold records of service for Naval Surgeons, there are also a number of records

of service volumes in ADM 104/166–9, and especially for temporary surgeons for the First World War period in ADM 104/170. Surgeons also appear in the *Medical Register*.

Records of Naval Pharmacists can be found in ADM 104/159.

*The Royal Marines*
Between 1899 and 1922, the Royal Marines were made up of the Royal Marine Light Infantry and the Royal Marine Artillery. The Royal Marine Light Infantry was split into divisions: Portsmouth, Plymouth and Chatham.

It is essential when researching Royal Marine other ranks to know their service number, as this will dictate which record series to consult. Apart from using ADM 313, the index of service records found in ADM 159, one easy way to find the service number of a marine who received any medals is to use the medal rolls in ADM 171. After 1885 all naval medal rolls indicate the service number of the recipient.

*ADM 157 Other Ranks*
Attestation and discharge papers for many marines, in both the Royal Marine Light

Infantry and the Royal Marine Artillery, can be found in this series. There is, however, a problem with this series. Some of the records are arranged by date of attestation, some by date of discharge and some by service number. It is therefore important to look very carefully when using ADM 157. Eventually it is hoped to create an effective index to the whole of this records series.

### ADM 159 Other Ranks

The records in ADM 159 are single-sheet records of service, bound into volumes and arranged by division and then in number order. This series is available on microfilm.

As a single-sheet record of service, the records in ADM 159 should provide date and place of birth; date of attestation; physical description; the company and the particular division in which the individual served; details of any sea service; and the name(s) of the ships on which he served. The records will indicate any medals he earned; whether the individual could swim; whether he was married, to whom and when; and, finally, when he was discharged.

## ADM 196 Officers

The records of service of officers of the Royal Marine Light Infantry and the Royal Marine Artillery can be found in the series ADM 196. There is a separate name index for these officers on the open shelves in the Microfilm Reading Room at the National Archives. As with many indexes, it provides volume and page number, the volume needing conversion into an ADM 196 reference. The conversion key is at the front of the index.

The records in ADM 196 will provide basic biographical details, such as where an individual served, whether at sea or ashore; details of any medals; and when the individual relinquished his commission.

## ADM 318 Women's Royal Naval Service Officers

Records of service of officers of the Women's Royal Naval Service are in the series ADM 316. Each officer is listed by name and can be searched for on the Catalogue.

The index of short service commissions for WRNS officers is in the series WO 321.

## ADM 336 Women's Royal Naval Service Ratings

The records of service of the Women's Royal Naval Service are arranged in service number order. ADM 336/1–22 is the name index, giving the service number, and ADM 336/23–9 the actual records. These have been digitized on DocumentsOnline and can be searched by name.

## The Queen Alexandra's Royal Naval Nursing Service

Records of service for full-time and reserve nurses of the Queen Alexandra's Royal Naval Nursing Service can be found in the series ADM 104/95 and 161–5. Records of Naval Massage Sisters are in ADM 104/171.

## The Royal Naval Reserve

The men who served in the Royal Naval Reserve were all from civilian seafaring jobs. They committed themselves to a period of service, whereby should the Admiralty need them they could be called upon for full-time service.

Not all of the records of service of the Royal Naval Reserve have survived. For the early existence of the Royal Naval Reserve the records are a very small sample, with greater chances of finding information about an officer than about a rating.

Royal Naval Reserve ratings committed themselves to the service for periods of four or five years. If they signed on they were given a new service number: it is therefore possible to look at a Royal Naval Reserve service number and tell an individual's specialization and whether he was on his first or a subsequent engagement.

For a full explanation of the Royal Naval Reserve service number system see *Naval Long Service Medals 1830–1990* by K.J. Douglas-Morris (Privately Published, 1991).

## BT 164 ROYAL NAVAL RESERVE, REPRESENTATIVE RECORDS OF SERVICE

The Royal Naval Reserve records in BT 164 are a very small sample. In many cases they represent but a part of a Royal Naval Reserve career, where the remainder may no longer survive.

## BT 377 ROYAL NAVAL RESERVE: RATINGS' RECORDS OF SERVICE (MICROFICHE COPIES)

By far the most significant collection of records of service of Royal Naval Reserve ratings are in BT 377. This series is arranged by service number, and each record contains information about the Merchant Navy service of an individual on one side and his Royal Naval Reserve or active service on the other.

There are two series of name indexes in BT 377, so it should be possible to identify an individual and his associated service number(s). Once you have located the number, you apply it to the remainder of BT 377.

Royal Naval Reserve service numbers are sometimes transposed, with the letter(s) moved from being a prefix to being a suffix. The records in BT 377 are arranged in letter sequence, and then each section is in number order. So if you have an Royal Naval Reserve service number, find the letters first and then the number.

If you find a Royal Naval Reserve rating's record of service and you know the individual served for more than five years, the record you find should be annotated with his previous and/or subsequent number(s).

ADM 240 ROYAL NAVAL RESERVE: OFFICERS' SERVICE RECORDS

Records of service of Royal Naval Reserve

officers can be found in the series ADM 240. This series is arranged by rank and date of seniority. The series covers Royal Naval Reserve officers commissioned from before the First World War up to the 1920s. As with most Royal Naval Reserve records, they will reflect both civil and military service.

To obtain the seniority date of a Royal Naval Reserve officer, use the *Navy List*.

## Royal Naval Volunteer Reserve

Unlike men of the Royal Naval Reserve, who were connected with the sea by their employment, men of the Royal Naval Volunteer Reserve were in most cases not employed as seafarers. Again unlike Royal Naval Reserve men, who were spread all around the coastline and who were called together as necessary, men of the Royal Naval Volunteer Reserve were collected together by regions (divisions) and specializations, and then in most cases employed throughout the Royal Navy fleet as and where applicable.

There were a number of different Royal Naval Volunteer Reserve divisions and specializations, some of which were only created between 1914 and 1918. Prior to 1914, many of the divisions were split into companies, and this can be reflected in the service number of Royal Naval Volunteer Reserve ratings. During the First World War anyone joining one of the Royal Naval Volunteer Reserve divisions already in existence had a 'Z' added after the first letter of his service number. The key Royal Naval Volunteer Reserve divisions were:

- Bristol
- Clyde
- London
- Mersey
- Sussex
- Tyne
- Wales.

The key specializations were:

- Anti-Aircraft
- Birmingham Electrical Engineers
- Mine Clearance Service.

The series ADM 337 Royal Naval Volunteer Reserve contains the records of service of

Royal Naval Volunteer Reserve ratings and most of the Royal Naval Volunteer Reserve officers. The ratings' records are arranged by division and then within that by number. There is a card index for Royal Naval Volunteer Reserve officers and this provides the volume and page number, the volume number requiring conversion into an ADM 337 piece reference.

Among the records in ADM 337 are two quite interesting series. The Mine Clearance Service was created only towards the end of the First World War and it included a number of ex-Royal Naval ratings. On a Mine Clearance Service record of service is sometimes noted the former Royal Naval official number of a rating. Most of the men of the Mine Clearance Service who had not already qualified for one were awarded a single British War Medal for the dangerous work clearing mines after the Armistice.

The Anti-Aircraft Corps of the Royal Naval Volunteer Reserve was created as a direct result of the early air attacks by Zeppelins on London, and they were employed manning anti-aircraft batteries and searchlight batteries in and around London. Many of those who served in this part of the Royal Naval Volunteer Reserve were over normal military age, and in many cases came from parts of society you would least expect. Judges, bankers, other legal professionals and newspaper employees, many over 50, saw service in the Anti-Aircraft Corps.

*Royal Naval Division*

Before the end of 1914 there was a surplus of sailors, for whom there were no ships. Winston Churchill decided to collect these men together to fight as soldiers on land, and so the Royal Naval Division was born.

Depending upon which part of the Royal Navy an individual originally came from (if at all), it may be possible to find part of the record of service in the records discussed above.

The operational control of the Royal Naval Division was transferred from the Admiralty to the War Office in 1916, and it is possible to find the records of service in the series already mentioned, as well as the following.

ADM 339 ROYAL NAVAL DIVISION: RECORDS OF SERVICE

This contains the record card records of

service kept by the Royal Naval Division themselves. Arranged in three alphabetical sequences – ratings, officers and those discharged dead – these records have been digitized and are available on DocumentsOnline. It is possible to search these records by name.

The records in this series are some of the most informative of all the First World War records of service as they are really a consolidated record taken from many different sources, created and circulated during the life of the Royal Naval Division.

### Naval officers: a final source

ADM 340

This file is called Royal Navy, Royal Naval Reserve, Royal Naval Volunteer Reserve and Women's Royal Naval Service: Officers' Service Record Cards and Files. It is a general series of records of service for all the officers of the naval services but not including the Royal Marines. This series is arranged in alphabetical order.

## Operational records

Many ships found in records of service or mentioned in the *Navy List* were not seagoing vessels but dockyards, training establishments and headquarters vessels. When you are searching for operational records with just a ship's name to go on, you may fail simply because the name is not that of a seagoing vessel.

In order to ascertain whether it really is a ship or a naval establishment, use:

- J.J. Colledge, *Ships of the Royal Navy* (Greenhill, 2003)
- Ben Warlow, *Shore Establishments of the Royal Navy* (Maritime Books, 1992).

The most obvious sources for operational information are ships' log books, but it is important to understand their purpose and shortcomings. The purpose of a log book was to record navigational information, ship's stores lost or damaged, disciplinary information and any key items that may have been recorded by the officer of the watch. Log books do not usually record operations in minute detail; this was the role of the 'Report of Proceedings'.

Log books can be found in the series

ADM 53. The easiest way to find a log is to search by name of ship and the year(s) on the Catalogue. Specifying the year(s) is very important, as the Royal Navy has used the same names for many ships over the last 300 years! Log books for submarines can be found in ADM 173.

Reports of Proceedings prior to 1914 can be found in the series ADM 1. Reports of Proceedings for the First World War period can be found in the records series ADM 137.

In order to locate a report between 1899 and 1918 it is necessary to begin with the series ADM 12. While this is a complicated process, it can be very rewarding: an explanatory leaflet is available, 'How to use ADM 12'.

When a particular naval action or operation resulted in a large quantity of papers being produced, these were frequently collected together in 'Cases'. Admiralty Case papers can be found in ADM 116.

### Records of campaign, long service and good conduct medals

Unlike the War Office medal records, where the campaign medal rolls are in WO 100 for all campaigns apart from the First World War and in WO 329 for the First World War, the Admiralty medal rolls for all campaign medals can be found in one series, ADM 171.

The records in ADM 171 include the campaign medals rolls for all medals issued to the naval services, but as you might expect they are arranged in different ways. Prior to the First World War, ADM 171 is arranged by campaign medal, with each roll arranged in alphabetical order by name of ship, with each roll in alphabetical order by name.

Among the medal rolls in ADM 171 for operations before the First World War are those for the following medals:

- the Queen's South Africa Medal;
- the China Medal 1900;
- the Africa General Service Medal 1902–56;
- the Naval General Service Medal 1915–62.

The campaign medal rolls for the First World War are arranged according to rank and service. The majority of medal rolls for officers are collected together and the rolls for ratings are split into the Royal Navy, the Royal Naval

Reserve, the Royal Naval Volunteer Reserve, the Royal Marines Light Infantry and the Royal Marines Artillery, with each being in alphabetical order.

Medals for long service and good conduct for the Royal Navy, the Royal Naval Reserve and the Royal Naval Volunteer Reserve can also be found in ADM 171, as can the medal roll for the Royal Fleet Reserve Long Service and Good Conduct Medal.

### Gallantry and meritorious service awards

Information about awards for gallantry and meritorious service can be found in a number of different series. Many recommendations for awards can be found in ADM 1, ADM 116 and ADM 137, and it is necessary to use ADM 12 in order to find them. A guide, 'How to Use ADM 12', can be obtained in the Research Enquiries Room.

During the First World War the Admiralty maintained an honours card index and this can be found in the Microfilm Reading Room. This card index not only tells you the award and when it was announced in *The London Gazette*, it will also tell you which 'Honours

Sheet' to consult for further information as to why the award was granted. The Honours Sheets are available in the series ADM 171 and are available on microfilm.

## Courts martial

All surviving Admiralty records concerning courts martial can be found in the series ADM 1 and ADM 156. Registers of courts martial for the Portsmouth and Plymouth Divisions of the Royal Marines can be found in the series ADM 194.

## Casualties

Although brief information about naval casualties may be found in a ship's log book, ADM 104/144 contains a register of those killed and wounded 1854–1911.

Other records concerning casualties and other deaths can be found in ADM 104/102, 103, 109, 110, 122, 125 and 140–3. Many of the deaths recorded in these volumes occurred during peacetime and were the result of accidents or disease.

First World War casualties can be found in ADM 242 Naval Casualties, Indexes, War Grave Rolls and Statistics Book, First World

War. The card index for naval officers is in the Research Enquiries Room.

Naval casualties are also listed in the Commonwealth War Graves Commission 'Debt of Honour' register at *www.cwgc.org*.

*Further reading*
See the following for more information:

MEDALS
William Spencer, *Medals: The Researcher's Guide* (The National Archives, 2006)

NAVAL RECORDS
Bruno Pappalardo, *Tracing Your Naval Ancestors* (Public Record Office, 2003)

## THE ROYAL AIR FORCE

Although the Royal Air Force was only formed on 1 April 1918, this section also covers the records of its forbears; the Royal Flying Corps and the Royal Naval Air Service.

Prior to the creation of the Royal Flying Corps in 1912, the responsibility for military aviation was in the hands of the Royal Engineers, in the guise of the Royal Engineers

Balloon Section. As the Royal Engineers was a corps of the British Army, information concerning records of service, operations and medals will be found in the Army section of this chapter on p. 44.

### Records of service

The records of service of members of the Royal Engineers Balloon Section will be found in WO 25 for officers and WO 97 for other ranks. The following advice concerns the records kept after 1913 and specifically after the creation of the RAF in 1918.

*Officers*
If an officer was commissioned into the Army and the Royal Flying Corps prior to 1 April 1918, you may find a record of service in WO 339 or WO 374. See the Army section on pp. 52–4.

The records of service of Royal Naval Air Service officers can be found in the series ADM 273. There is a name index for ADM 273, which provides the volume and page number where a record of service may be found. The volume number in the card index is the ADM 273 piece number.

The records of service of Royal Flying Corps and Royal Air Force officers who did not see service after 1921 can be found in the series AIR 76 Officers' Service Records. This series is available on microfilm and is arranged in alphabetical order. The series includes many officers of the Royal Flying Corps who were killed before the Royal Air Force came into existence, including Albert Ball VC.

Statements of officers' service may also be found in the squadron records in AIR 1. See 'Operational records' on p. 105.

*Airmen*

The records of service of men of the Royal Flying Corps who left the service prior to the creation of the Royal Air Force may be found in the First World War War Office records in WO 363 and WO 364. See pp. 44-50 for further information.

The records of service of the Royal Naval Air Service ratings, which provide information up to 31 March 1918, can be found in the series ADM 188. The official number of Royal Naval Air Service ratings was prefixed with the letter 'F'. See the Royal Navy ratings' record of service section on pp. 81–3 for further information.

The records of service of the Royal Air Force airmen can be found in the series AIR 79 and this series is arranged in service number order. Currently it is only the records of men with a number 329000 or lower that can be found in AIR 79. However, the record of service of any Royal Air Force airman who saw service in the Second World War and whose number is lower than 329000 will not be found in the series AIR 79.

A name index providing service number can be found in the series AIR 78. Please note that the index covers 1918–75, so it is important to remember that AIR 79 only includes numbers up to 329000.

If you have a Royal Air Force service number higher than 329000, the record of service is still held by the Royal Air Force. Frustratingly, this includes a large number of men of the Territorial Army who transferred into the Royal Flying Corps and then the Royal Air Force and who were given service numbers in the range starting 400000, but who saw nothing more than First World War service!

*Airwomen*

Surviving records of service of women who served in the Women's Royal Air Force in the First World War period can be found in the series AIR 80, but this only covers other ranks. No records of service for Women's Royal Air Force officers survive. AIR 80 is available on microfilm and is arranged in alphabetical order. The series is currently being digitized and when this process is completed the records will be available on DocumentsOnline.

## Operational records

The vast majority of operational records for squadrons of the Royal Flying Corps, the Royal Naval Air Service and the Royal Air Force can be found in the series AIR 1. The operational records in AIR 1 can be in the form of weekly reports, specific reports for certain operations and combat reports completed by individual pilots when they got back on the ground. Combat reports provide vivid details about air-to-air combat between aeroplanes.

Although it is possible to identify the operational reports of squadrons by keyword searching the Catalogue, at the front of the AIR 1 paper catalogue there is a list of flying units by brigade, wing or squadron, and this provides the pieces in AIR 1 where information about the records associated with that unit may be found. When using the squadron index it is important to note that prior to 1 April 1918 there were two number 1 squadrons, one Royal Flying Corps and one Royal Naval Air Service. When the Royal Air Force was created on 1 April 1918, the naval squadrons became the 200 series squadrons, so 1 Royal Naval Air Service became 201 Squadron Royal Air Force.

## Medals

There are currently only two key places to look for information about medals to the Royal Flying Corps/Royal Air Force. Recommendations for awards for gallantry and meritorious service may be found in the unit records in AIR 1. Recommendations and information about awards to members of the Royal Naval Air Service may be found in the naval records in ADM 116, ADM 137 and ADM 171.

Announcements concerning the award of the Royal Air Force Long Service and Good Conduct Medal during the reign of King

George V can be found in Air Ministry Orders in the series AIR 72.

Information about First World War campaign medals issued to the Royal Flying Corps may be in WO 329 and WO 372. See the section on campaign medals to the Army, pp.67–71.

Campaign medal information to members of the Royal Naval Air Service can be found in ADM 171. See the Royal Navy medal section, pp. 97–100.

Information about campaign medals can also be found on the record of service of an individual in either AIR 76 or AIR 79. Officers' records of service are usually stamped 'Services considered for grant of war medals'.

## Courts martial

The series AIR 21, which is the Register of Courts Martial, contains information about Royal Air Force personnel who were tried by court martial. The court martial records of Royal Flying Corps or Royal Naval Air Service personnel are discussed in the appropriate sections.

## Casualties

Details concerning casualties at unit level can be found in the unit records in AIR 1.

Information about Royal Naval Air Service casualties may be found in the ADM records mentioned in the Royal Navy casualty section, p. 100.

The officers of the Royal Flying Corps who died prior to 1 April 1918 are included in *Officers Died in the Great War*, access to which is available on CD-ROM or at the National Archives.

A published roll of honour which contains information about the flying services and their casualties can be found in *Airmen Died in the Great War, 1914–1918: The Roll of Honour of the British and Commonwealth Air Services of the First World War* by C. Hobson (Hayward, 1995)

Royal Air Force and associated casualties can be found on the Commonwealth War Graves Commission website, *www.cwgc.org*.

*Further reading*
See the following for more information:

RECORDS OF SERVICE
William Spencer, *Air Force Records: A Guide for Family Historians* (The National Archives, 2008)

MEDALS

William Spencer, *Medals: The Researcher's Guide* (The National Archives, 2006)

AIRCREW

T. Henshaw, *The Sky Their Battlefield* (Grub Street, 1995)

C. Shores, N. Franks and R. Guest, *Above the Trenches* (Grub Street, 1990)

## THE MERCHANT NAVY

It you think the records of the armed forces are complex, those of the Merchant Navy (formerly Mercantile Marine) can also be frustrating because of their complexity on the one hand and their lack of survival on the other!

If you really want to research a member of the Merchant Navy effectively I would recommend that you obtain a copy of either *Records of Merchant Shipping and Seamen* by K. Smith, C.T. Watts and M.J. Watts (Public Record Office, 1998) or *My Ancestor Was a Merchant Seaman* by C.T. and M.J. Watts (Federation of Family History Societies, 2002).

The following sources cover the Merchant

Navy in the 20th century, and they are the key and most easily used sources only.

### Records of service

Many of the records of service for merchant seaman serving prior to 1918 have not survived, and consequently attempts to find information about them can be unrewarding. The following records may or may not contain information on the merchant seaman you seek.

*Record cards*

BT 348      Register of Seamen, Central Index, Numerical Series (CR 2). This series covers seamen serving between 1921 and 1941 and also includes some of those serving prior to 1921. The series is arranged by 'Discharge A' number.

BT 349      Register of Seamen, Central Index, Alphabetical Series (CR 1). This series is similar to the above but is arranged in alphabetical order.

BT 350      Register of Seamen, Special Index, Alphabetical Series (CR 10). This series covers the period 1918–21 and is arranged in alphabetical order.

BT 364          This contains record cards extracted from
                the above three series.

*Crew and agreements*
When a merchant seaman joined a ship, he
'signed on' in a formal agreement. These
agreements, which list the crew of a given
ship at a given date, can be found in a number
of different series. For the periods 1861–1912
and 1913–23, a sample of these agreements
can be found in the series BT 99. A small number of agreements for famous ships can be
found in BT 100.

   For the period of the First World War, agreements and log books can be found in BT 165,
and these are arranged in order of the ship's
official number and by year.

*Registers of masters' and mates' certificates
of competency*
There are a number of registers of certificates of
competency for a variety of different officer specializations of the merchant service for service
trading in home waters (HT), foreign waters (FT)
and in the colonies (C), and these can be found
in many different BT records series.

The following, with the date range they cover, may be of use.

| | |
|---|---|
| BT 122 1845–1906 | Registers: Masters and Mates: FT |
| BT 123 1881–1921 | Registers: Masters and Mates of Steamships: FT |
| BT 125 1845–1921 | Registers: Masters and Mates: HT |
| BT 128 1870–1921 | Registers: Masters and Mates: C |
| BT 129 1880–1921 | Registers: Skippers and Mates of Fishing Boats |
| BT 130 1883–1922 | Registers: Skippers and Mates of Fishing Boats |
| BT 138 1880–1917 | Index to BT 129 and BT 130 |
| BT 139 1861–1921 | Registers of Engineers |
| BT 140 1870–1921 | Registers of Engineers |
| BT 142 1861–1921 | Registers of Engineers |
| BT 141 1861–1921 | Indexes to BT 139, BT 140 and BT 142 |
| BT 317/1–7 1917–68 | Register of Masters' and Mates' Certificates, Passing and Renewals |
| BT 352/1 1910–30 | Index to Certificates of Competency: Masters. Mates, Engineers and Fishing Officers |

Information about Merchant Navy captains may also be found in *Lloyd's Captains' Register 1851–1947*, a copy of which can be found on microfilm in the Microfilm Reading Room.

## Operational records

Information about merchant ships and their encounters with the German and Turkish navies during the First World War can be found in the operational records of the Royal Navy in the series ADM 137 (see pp. 95–7).

Brief information about operational matters can sometimes be found in BT 165 Registrar General of Shipping and Seamen and Predecessor: Ships' Official Logs, but only if the ship was not lost.

## Medals

Prior to the First World War and within the date range covered by this guide, the only campaign medal awarded to officers of the Merchant Navy was the Transport Medal, which was given to the masters and senior officers of those merchant vessels that took troops and equipment to fight in South Africa in 1899–1902 and to China in 1900. The medal roll for the Transport Medal can be found in ADM 171/52.

The medal records for members of the Merchant Navy who qualified for First World

War campaign medals can be found in the series BT 351 Registrar General of Shipping and Seamen: Index of First World War Mercantile Marine Medals and the British War Medal. This series is arranged in alphabetical order and is available on microfiche. The information this series will give you includes not only the medal entitlement but also the date and place of birth of an individual and – perhaps just as important and very useful for looking at other records – a man's Discharge A number.

Information about awards for gallantry and meritorious service can be found in the series BT 261, and this series is arranged in chronological order.

Information about merchant seamen who received the Distinguished Service Cross or Distinguished Service Medal may be found in the series ADM 137. See the information on awards for gallantry and meritorious service in the Royal Navy section, p. 99.

### Casualties

Information concerning the loss of merchant ships can sometimes be found in ADM 137. It is necessary to use the series ADM 12 to find these. A leaflet, 'How to Use ADM 12', is available upon request.

The series BT 339 Registrar General of Shipping and Seamen: Rolls of Honour, Wars of 1914–18 and 1939–45 may also be of use.

Merchant seamen are also found on the Commonwealth War Graves Commission website, *www.cwgc.org*.

*Further reading*
See the following for more information:

RECORDS OF SERVICE
K. Smith, C.T. Watts and M.J. Watts, *Records of Merchant Shipping and Seamen* (Public Record Office, 1998)

MEDALS
William Spencer, *Medals: The Researcher's Guide* (The National Archives, 2006)

## SQUADRONS.

*No. 58 (Bomber) Squadron*—contd.

*Flg. Offs.*

| | |
|---|---|
| David A. Craik [s] | 14Aug.29 |
| Arthur T. Orchard | 14Dec.29 |
| Charles S. Gill [p] | 12Feb.30 |
| Thomas H. Wilson | 12Feb.30 |
| George F. Humphries | 3May32 |
| Francis C. Allen | 16Nov.31 |
| George E. S. Williams | 17June30 |
| James O. Wills | 20June32 |

*Pilot Off.*

| | |
|---|---|
| Robert G. Coventry | 17Dec.32 |

*Warrant Officer—2nd Class.*

| | |
|---|---|
| George H. Eyles | 12Jan.33 |

*8 Airman Pilots.*

### No. 60 (BOMBER) SQUADRON.

H.Q. and 3 Flights. Wapiti.
No. 1 (Indian Wing) Station.
Kohat.

*Sqdn. Ldr.*

| | |
|---|---|
| Arthur D. Pryor | 8Jan.33 |

*Flight Lieuts.*

| | |
|---|---|
| Cecil H. Harrison | 24Jan.32 |
| Edmund A. C. Britton, *D.F.C.* | 21Sept.31 |
| Geoffrey C. Stemp | 16Oct31 |

*Flg. Offs.*

| | |
|---|---|
| Herbert M. B. Collins | 9Apr.30 |
| Maurice W. S. Robinson | 4Apr.32 |
| William G. A. Coulson | 11Oct.32 |
| Peter H. Hamley | 7Feb.33 |
| Derek Addenbrooke | 17June32 |
| Richard H. Younghusband | 10Dec.32 |

*Pilot Off.*

| | |
|---|---|
| Anthony D. Isemonger | 2Nov.32 |

*6 Airman Pilots.*

### No. 70 (BOMBER TRANSPORT) SQUADRON.

H.Q. and 2 Flights. Victoria.
' Iraq Command.
Hinaidi.

*Wing Cdr.*

| | |
|---|---|
| George C. Bailey, *D.S.O., p.s.a.* | 18Mar.32 |

*Sqdn. Ldrs.*

| | |
|---|---|
| Ernest J. Cuckney, *D.S.C.* | 1Oct.32 |
| George T. Richardson | 4Mar.32 |

*Flight Lieuts.*

| | |
|---|---|
| John H. C. Wake | 13Sept.31 |
| George D. Harvey | 23Jan.32 |
| Patrick V. Williams | 4Oct.32 |
| Patrick de C. Festing Smith | 1Apr.33 |

*Flg. Offs.*

| | |
|---|---|
| Guy H. A. Blackwood [p] | 23Jan.32 |
| Ian L. S. McNicol | 23Jan.32 |
| Herbert R. Clay | 11July30 |
| John P. Mansfield | 27Jan.33 |

*Flg. Offs.*—contd.

| | |
|---|---|
| William E. Hooper | 27Jan.33 |
| Maurice R. D. Trewby | 28Feb.33 |
| John A. Dobson | 27Jan.33 |
| Bernard A. Casey | 16Oct.31 |
| Lennox S. Lamb | 8Feb.33 |
| Harry L. Tancred | 16Oct.31 |
| William Pickersgill | 3Jan.33 |
| George H. Denholm | 28Feb.33 |

*Pilot Offs.*

| | |
|---|---|
| Malcolm F. Calder | 29Aug.32 |
| John N. H. Whitworth | 28Feb.33 |

*Stores Branch.*
*Flg. Off.*

| | |
|---|---|
| James E. Reynolds | 26Jan.32 |

*Warrant Officers—2nd Class.*

| | |
|---|---|
| William Shaw | 31Oct.30 |
| George D. Merron | 17Feb.32 |
| George G. Meager | 10Mar.32 |
| Arthur Wordon | 11Nov.31 |

*8 Airman Pilots.*

### No. 84 (BOMBER) SQUADRON.

H.Q. and 3 Flights. Wapiti.
' Iraq Command.
Shaibah.

*Flight Lieuts.*

| | |
|---|---|
| Robert J. Rodwell | 8Feb.33 |
| Edward E. Arnold, *D.F.C.* | 6May32 |
| Cyril Walter | 4Oct.32 |
| Arthur D. Rogenhagen | 2Jan.31 |

*Flg. Offs.*

| | |
|---|---|
| Wilfred S. C. Adams | 3Nov.31 |
| Hurll F. Chester | 26Sept.31 |
| Jeffrey H. Supple [p] | 4Oct.32 |
| Leonard J. Crosbie | 23Jan.32 |
| Guy A. Bolland | 23Jan.32 |
| Thomas A. Jefferson | 12June31 |
| Eric W. Whitley | 13Nov.31 |
| David Sloan | 4Apr.32 |
| Cedric W. Williams | 28Feb.33 |
| William W. Stainthorpe | 28Feb.33 |

*Pilot Offs.*

| | |
|---|---|
| Thomas C. Chambers | 2Nov.32 |
| Arthur Franklin | 20Mar.33 |

*6 Airman Pilots.*

*Stores Branch.*
*Flg. Off.*

| | |
|---|---|
| Roland G. Seymour | 1Oct.32 |

*Accountant Branch.*
*Flg. Offs.*

| | |
|---|---|
| Maurice L. Jones | 26Oct.31 |
| Percival Griffiths | 10Feb.33 |

*Education Officer.*
*Grade III.*

| | |
|---|---|
| Percy H. Legg, *Esq., B.Sc.* | 19Aug.32 |

*Warrant Officer.*

| | |
|---|---|
| Edward W. Walker | 24Feb.32 |

*Warrant Officers—2nd Class.*

| | |
|---|---|
| Maurice Caulfield | 13Feb.32 |
| Frederick Williams | 28Oct.32 |

Chapter 2

# The inter-war years: 1919–39

- Operational records
  *The Army*
  *The Royal Navy*
  *The Royal Air Force*
- Medals, awards, courts martial and casualties
  *Campaign medals*
  *Long service medals*
  *Coronation and Jubilee medals*
  *Gallantry and meritorious service awards*
  *Courts martial*
  *Casualties*
- The Merchant Navy

## SETTING THE SCENE

Many in the armed forces felt that they would eventually return to the same type of peace-time roles that they had been undertaking before 1914. Although the sizes of the three services were dramatically reduced, they were not idle. The innovations of the First World War years were put to good use in dealing with many of the pre-war problems, such as unruly and disaffected peoples throughout many parts of the empire.

Operations in Iran, Iraq, Russia, Turkey, Somaliland, India, Burma and Palestine all took place at various times in the period between 12 November 1918 and 2 September 1939.

Although very few records of service are available for the inter-war period, those that are available really concern individuals who, in most cases, started their service prior to 1919, and who have already been mentioned in the preceding chapter. This is not to say you will not find information about an individual between 1918 and 1939, it is just that the key biographical information is still retained in most cases by the Ministry of Defence. There are many ways of gathering information about an individual who served between 1918 and 1939: it just takes time and effort to go through every available source.

The information available for the inter-war period falls into two categories: operational records and some medal records. However, it is still possible to find out about individuals in some depth during this period, for example by looking for information about officers from the *Navy List, Army List* and *Air Force List*.

## OPERATIONAL RECORDS

Many of the operational record formats used in the period 1899–1918 continued into the inter-war period. There are, however, a few new record series which, while they were in existence towards the end of the First World War, really come into more general use between 1919 and 1939.

### The Army

Operations conducted by the Army in various parts of the world, most notably in Russia, Iraq (Mesopotamia), Iran (Persia) and on the North West Frontier of India, are all recorded in the war diaries in WO 95.

Further reports by officers commanding various operations can be found in the series WO 32, WO 33 and WO 106. The easiest way to locate them is to search the Catalogue by keyword, using either the place where the operation(s) took place or the name of the officer commanding the operation.

A series of war diaries for operations conducted between the wars in such places as India, Burma and Palestine can be found in the series WO 191. The most effective way to locate these is to search by place or unit.

Detailed despatches concerning operations were published in *The London Gazette*. It is possible to search for these online at *www.gazettes-online.co.uk*. I suggest searching by the author of the despatch, usually the officer commanding, or the place where the operation(s) took place.

Published campaign and unit histories are always full of information, but it depends upon the status and activities of an individual as to whether they will be mentioned. Many unit histories are available in the library at the National Archives.

### The Army List

The Army List has been published in various forms since the 18th century and its purpose has always been to list officers holding commissions in the Army at the time of publication.

Army Lists for the period 1899–1953 come in a variety of forms depending on the frequency of publication. The arrangement of the Lists varies but there are some constants. Each has a name index for each officer mentioned, and the index entry will tell you on which page, or pages, information about the officer may be found. A typical entry will provide the regiment/corps the individual was serving in at the time of publication, their rank and any post-nominal letters indicating awards and qualifications.

Some of the Army Lists published on a quarterly basis may have a section called 'War Services'. In this section, arranged in alphabetical order, you will find brief details about an officer's operational service and any medals he may have been awarded.

Depending upon the date, most Army Lists will include officers of the Regular Army, Militia, Volunteers, Territorial Army, Dominion forces, Imperial Yeomanry and Indian Army. The Indian Army also had its own List, copies of which for the period 1902–39 can be found in the National Archives' library.

Although the Army List does contain details concerning officers, Warrant Officers 1st Class may also be found in the List up to the 1930s. Apart from a list of Warrant Officers, the January edition of an Army List may also include a list of Warrant Officers in receipt of a pension, and the List will tell you when the individual retired.

## The Royal Navy

Log books of ships serving between the wars can still be found in the series ADM 53, and those for submarines in ADM 173. It is possible to find Reports of Proceedings in ADM 1 and ADM 116. A few reports of naval activities prior to the outbreak of the Second World War can be found in the series ADM 199.

If you are unable to find a log for a ship, you may find that you are dealing with a naval establishment and not a seagoing vessel. Look in the following two books, as they will help you ascertain a ship's status:

- J.J. Colledge, *Ships of the Royal Navy* (Greenhill, 2003)
- Ben Warlow, *Shore Establishments of the Royal Navy* (Maritime Books, 1992).

Examples of operational records for between the wars include ADM 116, 3036, 3690 and 4312 for operations off Palestine. The *Navy List* may also help.

## The Royal Air Force

The key areas of operation for the Royal Air

Force between 1918 and 1939 were Somaliland, India and Burma, Palestine and Mesopotamia (Iraq). The Royal Air Force was also involved in operations in the Sudan and in flights of exploration over many parts of the world.

Operational records for the Royal Air Force for the period between the wars can be found in a number of different records series. Of these, the series AIR 27 really starts to be used more effectively and can be very informative.

AIR 27 (Operational Record Books) is arranged in squadron number order and is available on microfilm. The series covers all Royal Air Force operational squadrons and lists the flights undertaken by the squadron, who flew in the aircraft and the task they carried out. Unfortunately the records are mostly concerned with the aircrew, although it is possible to find non-flying members of a squadron mentioned, usually in the appendices when the squadron is moving bases.

The *Air Force List* for the inter-war period can be very useful, as it will tell you the names of officers serving in a squadron and where they were based.

Other Royal Air Force operational records can be found in the series AIR 2, AIR 5, AIR 8 and AIR 23. Information on Royal Air Force operations in India, for example, can be found in AIR 5/1321–2 and 1329–37. Reports on Royal Air Force operations in Iraq can be found in AIR 5/724 and 1253–5 and 1287–94, and in AIR 23/249–53. Details on Palestine operations conducted by the Royal Air Force can be found in AIR 5/1243–8.

Some Royal Air Force operations in the immediate post-First World War period were carried out by specially created units – for example, Z Force was created for operations in Somaliland – and it may be necessary to search the Catalogue for these units or the places where they operated.

## MEDALS, AWARDS, COURTS MARTIAL AND CASUALTIES

Although millions of medals were issued for the First World War, service personnel continued to receive other medals for campaign service, gallantry and meritorious service and for long service and good conduct.

## Campaign medals

Many campaign medal rolls for operational service between the wars are still being transferred to the National Archives from the Ministry of Defence. The following information is as up to date as it can be but is likely to change.

*The Army*
Rolls for campaign medals for operations after the First World War can be found in the series WO 100, and these include the following:

the Africa General Service Medal 1902–56;
the Indian General Service Medal 1908–35;
the Indian General Service Medal 1936–9;
the General Service Medal 1918–62.

The following operations are covered:

Somaliland 1920;
Afghanistan North West Frontier 1919;
Waziristan 1919–21 and 1921–4;
Mahsud 1919–20;
Malabar 1921–2;
North West Frontier 1930–1;
Burma 1930–2;
Mohmand 1933;
North West Frontier 1939;
South Persia;

Kurdistan;
Iraq;
North West Persia;
Southern Desert: Iraq;
Palestine;
North West Frontier 1936–7;
North West Frontier 1937–9.

## The Royal Navy

Unlike the Army, there are very few medal rolls for naval operations after 1918. The rolls available are for operations off Somaliland in 1920, in ADM 171/64, and operations in Iran and Iraq, in ADM 171/62.

## The Royal Air Force

The only post-First World War Royal Air Force medal roll currently available is that for Somaliland 1920, and it can be found in AIR 2/2267–70.

Where available, information about post-First World War campaign medals may be found on an airman's record of service in AIR 79.

## Long service medals

Long service and good conduct medals awarded to members of the Army were announced in Army Orders and these can be found in the series WO 123. Future medal rolls for the Army Long Service and Good Conduct Medal will be in WO 102.

Medal rolls for long service and good conduct medals to the naval forces can be found in ADM 171. These rolls include medals to the Royal Navy and Royal Marines, separate rolls for the Royal Naval Reserve and the Royal Naval Volunteer Reserve, and rolls for the Royal Fleet Reserve.

Royal Air Force long service and good conduct medals were announced in Air Ministry Orders and these can be found in the series AIR 72. However, they only cover awards granted during the reign of King George V.

### Coronation and Jubilee medals

Alphabetical lists of both military and civil recipients of the 1935 Jubilee Medal and the 1937 Coronation Medal can be found in the library at the National Archives.

### Gallantry and meritorious service awards

All awards for gallantry and meritorious service were announced in *The London Gazette*, now online at *www.gazettes-online.co.uk*, and this is the best place to start your research. In many cases the announcement in *The London Gazette* will be all the information you are able to find.

Access to *The London Gazette* in digital form and in hard copy in the series ZJ 1 is available at the National Archives.

*The Army*
A few recommendations for awards granted for services in Waziristan between 1919 and 1924 can be found in WO 32/5428 and 5429. Other recommendations for awards prior to the Second World War can be found in the series WO 373.

*The Royal Navy*
Recommendations for awards to naval personnel involved in operations in the Baltic in 1919 can be found in ADM 137/1683. These awards were announced in *The London Gazette* on 8 March 1920.

A file containing recommendations for awards for the Wanhsien Incident in 1926 can be found in ADM 116/2497.

Other files concerning awards granted as part of the New Year or Birthday Honours Lists can be found in ADM 1 and ADM 116.

*The Royal Air Force*
Perhaps an illustration of how many operations were carried out by the Royal Air Force between the wars is the number of files concerning awards granted to the service, from recommendations for awards to the Z Unit for Somaliland in AIR 2/204 to recommendations for awards for operations in Waziristan between 1937 and 1939 in AIR 2/2516 and AIR 2/9404. A much more complete list of files concerning awards to the Royal Air Force for operations, long-distance flights and New Year and Birthday Honours Lists can be found in *Medals: The Researcher's Guide* by William Spencer (The National Archives, 2006).

## Courts martial

Courts martial records for the three armed services are in most cases in the same records series as those mentioned in Chapter 1. To get blow-by-blow proceedings of a court martial is very unusual, as not all have been selected for preservation. The following records are arranged and listed according to service.

## The Army

Proceedings of army courts martial are in the series WO 71 and the registers of Field General Courts Martial and Military Courts can be found in WO 213.

Other registers of courts martial include;

| | |
|---|---|
| WO 86 | District Courts Martial, Home and Abroad |
| WO 88 | District Courts Martial, India |
| WO 90 | General Courts Martial, Abroad |
| WO 92 | General Courts Martial, Home |

## The Royal Navy

All surviving records of naval courts martial are in ADM 156 and ADM 178. Registers of courts martial for the Portsmouth and Plymouth Division Royal Marines can be found in ADM 194.

## The Royal Air Force

The Royal Air Force registers of courts martial are in the series AIR 21 and the charge books are in AIR 43.

## Casualties

Information concerning casualties that occurred between 1919 and 2 September 1939 can frequently be found in the operational records mentioned above. Only the Admiralty kept information about their casualties in one record source, and these can be found in ADM 104.

The dates of death of officers of the Army, Royal Navy and Royal Air Force can usually be found in the casualty sections of the *Army, Navy* and *Air Force Lists*.

It is sometimes possible to find information in *The Times* newspaper, access to the digitized version of which is available at the National Archives.

## THE MERCHANT NAVY

Although the Merchant Navy between the wars was not involved in warlike activities, its records are mentioned in Chapters 1 and 3 because of war service in the First and Second World Wars. It is appropriate to link these periods together with information in this section to maintain continuity. Many Merchant Navy personnel saw service in both world wars and, of course, between them, and it would be inappropriate to exclude an important series of records.

Unlike the armed forces, where almost all of the records of service for the period are still with the Ministry of Defence, the records of service for the Merchant Navy can be found at the National Archives in the series BT 372.

The record for each merchant seaman in the series BT 372 is listed by name and can be searched for on the Catalogue by name, date and place of birth, and Discharge A number. Perhaps one of the best things about the series BT 372 is the fact that in most cases you will find a photograph of the subject individual.

*Further reading*
See the following for more information:

THE ROYAL NAVY AND ROYAL MARINES
Bruno Pappalardo, *Tracing Your Naval Ancestors* (Public Record Office, 2003)

THE ROYAL AIR FORCE
William Spencer, *Air Force Records: A Guide for Family Historians* (The National Archives, 2008)

MERCHANT SEAMEN
K. Smith, C.T. Watts and M.J. Watts, *Records of Merchant Shipping and Seamen* (Public Record Office, 1998)

MEDALS
William Spencer, *Medals: The Researcher's Guide* (The National Archives, 2006)

## 2nd HUNTINGDONSHIRE BATTALION

### Lt.-Colonel

| | |
|---|---|
| Wilson, W. E., <u>D.S.O.</u> | 1/ 2/41 |

### Majors

| | |
|---|---|
| Gotobed, E. A. | 1/ 2/41 |
| Hunnybun, K., <u>D.S.O.</u> | 1/ 2/41 |
| Raby, H. | 1/ 2/41 |
| Standen, F. A. | 1/ 2/41 |
| Burgess, T. H. | 10/ 4/42 |
| Yarnold, W. H. | 1/ 4/42 |
| Fenescall, W. J. | 9/ 9/42 |

### Captains

| | |
|---|---|
| Ashpole, G. W., <u>M.M.</u> | 1/ 2/41 |
| Cannon, C. H. | 17/ 3/42 |
| Davies, J. J. | 9/ 9/42 |
| Maule, E. G. F. | 1/12/42 |
| | 11/ 9/41 |
| Tyson, W. P. | 1/12/42 |
| Braybrooke, J. E. | 4/ 6/43 |
| Loworth, J. S. | 5/11/43 |
| Corbett, B. P. | 14/12/43 |

### Lieutenants

| | |
|---|---|
| Muller, A. C. | 1/ 2/41 |
| Jarvis, A. E. | 1/ 2/41 |
| Jarvis, N. W. | 1/ 2/41 |
| Knights, J. A. | 1/ 2/41 |
| Fenton, P. L. | 1/ 2/41 |
| Mansfield, A. J. | 1/ 2/41 |
| Mansfield, G. H. | 1/ 2/41 |
| Mulcaster, S. | 1/ 2/41 |
| Huston, E. O. | 1/ 2/41 |
| Storey, A. R. H. | 1/ 2/41 |
| Waller-Stevens, L. J. | 1/ 2/41 |
| Rocker, J. | 1/ 2/41 |
| Davies, A. F. | 25/11/41 |
| Hicks, W. S. | 29/11/41 |
| Cresswell, H. | 1/ 1/42 |
| Chapman, E. | 4/ 4/42 |
| Kinding, A. L. | 1/ 9/42 |
| Kallsworth, H. M., <u>C.B.E.</u> | 10/ 9/42 |
| Kowe, S. E. | 10/ 9/42 |
| Wight, D. B. | 12/ 9/42 |
| Neal, R. M. S. | 6/11/42 |
| Kemp, H. W. | 1/12/42 |
| Clarke, C. | 4/ 6/43 |

### Lieutenants - contd.

| | |
|---|---|
| Dunkley, W. T. J. | 1/ |
| Arkley, J. E. | 7/ |
| Horrex, J. R. | 6/ |

### 2nd Lieutenants

| | |
|---|---|
| Gurry, F. H. | 4/ |
| Smithies, J. F. | 11/ |
| D'Oyly, H. F. | 26/ |
| Lenton, R. G. | 26/ |
| Disney, F. H. | 26/ |
| Creatorex, A. P. | 26/ |
| Tiffin, G. | 26/ |
| Rose, R. S. | 26/ |
| Headley, H. | 20/ |
| Tunnacliffe, W. R. | 12/ |
| White, F. W. | 12/ |
| Price, O. H. | 17/1 |
| Lee, W. C. | 5/ |
| Parker, M. P. | 18/ |
| Stiles, R. H. | 12/ |
| Varley, A. W. | 4/ |
| Bitten, S. | 17/ |
| Telfer, G. E. | 8/1 |
| Thompson, P. | 6/1 |

### Adjutant

| | |
|---|---|
| James, Capt. (temp. 12/7/41) | |
| W. A., Gen. List Inf. | 12/ |

### Captain for Administrative & Quarter Master Duties

| | |
|---|---|
| Roder, Capt. (<u>actg.</u> 9/5/43) | |
| J. H., <u>M.M.</u>, K.R.R.C. | 9/ |

### Medical Officers

| | |
|---|---|
| Doubble, Maj. M. S. | 15/ |
| Musson, Capt. J. A. W., <u>M.B.</u> | 12/ |
| Greenwood, Capt. A. A. | 12/ |

Chapter 3

# The Second World War: 1939–45

- Operational records
  *The Army*
  *The Royal Navy*
  *The Royal Marines*
  *The Royal Air Force*
  *Combined Operations*
- Special Operations Executive
- Medals, gallantry and meritorious service awards
- Casualties
- Prisoners of war
- Courts martial
- The Merchant Navy
- The Home Front
  *The Home Guard*
  *The Women's Land Army*
  *Conscientious objectors*

## SETTING THE SCENE

As we saw in Chapter 2, there are very few more recent records of service available as most are still retained by the Ministry of Defence. There are however, plenty of records that will keep you busy, as long as you have the information available to unlock them.

In order to make best use of the records discussed in this chapter, the more specific the unit details you have, the easier it will be to locate the right records. For example, if you only know that an individual served in the Royal Artillery in the Second World War, you are not going to get very far. If you know that a man was a gunner with 9 Medium Regiment, Royal Artillery in 1942, you are going to be more successful.

The same can work for the operational records of the Royal Navy and the Royal Air Force. Just knowing that someone was in the Royal Navy or the Royal Air Force is not sufficient: a ship or squadron is needed to proceed further.

If you have the record of service of a person who saw service in the Second World War or more recently, the information contained within it will help you use the records at the National Archives.

There was a huge expansion of the armed forces in 1939–45 with the reintroduction of conscription. Even after the Second World War ended in Europe, the war continued in the Far East for almost four more months.

Not only can you find out about the records of the armed forces, but also the Home Guard, the Merchant Navy, certain aspects of Civil Defence and the Special Operations Executive.

A significant number of operations conducted during the Second World War were given specific codenames, such as Dynamo (the evacuation of Dunkirk), Biting (the Bruneval raid) and Overlord (the D Day landings). It is possible to search the Catalogue using operational codenames.

The way operational records of the Army were kept after the Second World War means that at least two different series will need to be consulted to obtain operational information.

## OPERATIONAL RECORDS

Unlike many of the operational records for preceding periods, the records for the Second

World War may contain information about the activities of more than one service. This is especially so where operations were conducted by one or more service in conjunction with another.

Once you have exhausted the operational records of the specific service you are researching, you may need to look at the records of one of the other services.

### The Army

Unlike the Unit War Diaries for the First World War, which can be found in one series (WO 95), the operational records of units in the Second World War are arranged according to operational theatre, with the Unit War Diaries being in one series and the Headquarters Papers being in another. This makes researching the activities of one unit throughout the whole war very complicated and time-consuming.

The purpose of Unit War Diaries was to record the activities of a given unit on a daily basis. Beyond stating where the unit was, they should also tell you what the unit was doing. Second World War diaries mention other ranks far less that those of the First World War period.

Most diaries of a battalion or equivalent contain periodic lists of officers serving in that unit, so they can be very useful for following the movements and postings of an officer.

Each series of war diaries contains diaries for the in-theatre high command at General Headquarters, army, corps, division and brigade level, as well as subordinate units.

The arrangement varies for each of the records series containing the Second World War war diaries. In most cases the arrangement is by hierarchy, with the Headquarters listed first, then the army command, then corps, then divisions and then brigades.

In most cases the infantry diaries are grouped together, as are those of the cavalry and the other corps. Each of these sections is then arranged either in regimental order of precedence or, in the case of the corps, by unit type and then in numerical order. So, for example, all of the light anti-aircraft units of the Royal Artillery are together, and these are then arranged in numerical order.

All the diaries in each of the following series

are listed in chronological ranges as well as in the sequences as described above. Therefore, if the unit you are interested in remained in the same operational theatre, you will need to look for a diary for each year they were there, as the Second World War diaries are arranged quite differently from most diaries in WO 95.

As already stated, Second World War Unit War Diaries are arranged by operational theatre, and these are as follows:

| | |
|---|---|
| WO 166 | Home Forces: War Diaries |
| WO 167 | British Expeditionary Force, France: War Diaries |
| WO 168 | British North West Expeditionary Force, Norway: War Diaries |
| WO 169 | British Forces, Middle East: War Diaries |
| WO 170 | Central Mediterranean Forces (British Element): War Diaries |
| WO 171 | Allied Expeditionary Force, North West Europe (British Element): |
| WO 172 | British and Allied Land Forces, South East Asia: War Diaries |
| WO 173 | West African Command: War Diaries |
| WO 174 | British Forces, Madagascar: War Diaries |
| WO 175 | Allied Forces, North Africa (British Element) |
| WO 176 | British Forces, Various Smaller Theatres |
| WO 177 | Army Medical Services: War Diaries |

The diaries in WO 177 cover all operational theatres and are arranged by the different type of medical unit, such as hospitals and field ambulances.

In WO 218 can be found Unit War Diaries of the Long Ranger Desert Group, Special Air Service, commando units, special service brigades and independent companies.

Failure to locate some diaries in what may seem the appropriate series can be explained by the fact that many units may have started in one place and then moved to another. For example, many of the forces used for the invasion of Sicily and Italy came from North Africa and the Middle East, and it may therefore be necessary to look in WO 175 and WO 169 before looking in WO 170.

The Military Headquarters Papers for the various operational theatres are listed below. The vast majority of the papers do not mention individuals by name but they do contain plenty about operations, their planning and execution.

WO 199    Military Headquarters Papers: Home Forces
WO 201    Military Headquarters Papers: Middle East

| WO 203 | Military Headquarters Papers: South East Asia |
| WO 204 | Military Headquarters Papers: Mediterranean Forces |
| WO 205 | Military Headquarters Papers: 21 Army Group |
| WO 219 | Supreme Headquarters Allied Expeditionary Force: HQ Papers |

**The Royal Navy**

As with preceding sections, ship's log books can be found in the series ADM 53 and submarine logs in ADM 173.

Reports of Proceedings may be found in ADM 199. To locate these, use the Ships Card Index in the Research Enquiries Room. It is also possible to find many reports from individual ships, and reports of the sinking of many ships, in the series ADM 1 and ADM 116.

Details concerning the many hundreds of convoys of the Second World War can be found in ADM 237 and ADM 199. It is possible to search the Catalogue by convoy number.

Large quantities of paperwork collected together around one subject were known as Admiralty Cases and these can be found in ADM 116. There are many files on operational matters in ADM 116.

The naval papers used at the end of the Second World War to write the official history can be found in the series ADM 199 War History Cases and Papers. There are a large number of files concerning all aspects of naval operations, and the series can be searched by subject, operational codename or by name of vessel. The Ships Card Index, available in the Research Enquiries Room, can be used to find records in ADM 199.

A separate index of papers in ADM 199 concerning Operation Neptunc, the naval side of the Normandy landings, is available as a supplementary finding aid in the Research Enquiries Room.

## The Royal Marines

The Unit War Diaries of Royal Marine Commandos and other units can be found in the series ADM 202.

## The Royal Air Force

During the Second World War it was the Royal Air Force that took the war to Germany before the D Day landings in June 1944. This fact is ably illustrated by the fact that the Distinguished

## The *Navy List*

As with the *Army List*, the *Navy List* for the same period is arranged in a number of different ways, but there are constants. In all *Navy Lists* there are always alphabetical lists of active officers of the Royal Navy and the Royal Marines, and some contain alphabetical lists of retired officers.

Entries for officers on the active list give rank, seniority and where serving, as either a numerical code or an abbreviation. The numerical codes relate to ships and these can be found in the *List* in alphabetical order. Each ship then lists all its officers and their duty in that ship. Abbreviated entries in the active list usually relate to non-seagoing appointments, and a key to these can be found in the *Lists*.

Entries for officers listed as retired give a page number on which will be found their highest rank and the seniority date at that rank.

As the Royal Navy grew, so too did the Royal Naval Reserve and then the Royal Naval Volunteer Reserve. Officers of the Royal Naval Reserve and Royal Naval Volunteer Reserve also have their own separate alphabetical lists within the *Navy List*.

Warrant Officers such as Boatswains, Gunners and Carpenters are included in the *Navy List*, as are the Australian, Canadian, New Zealand and Royal Indian navies. For the period of the Second World War senior civil officers of the Admiralty are also included in the *List*.

Flying Cross was the most common gallantry award granted during the war, with just over 20,000 being awarded.

There are many printed sources concerning the activities of the Royal Air Force in the Second World War and some are available in the library at the National Archives. The records listed below are the key sources where information may be found about Royal Air Force operations and personnel, but as is usually the case with the Royal Air Force, the vast majority of people mentioned in the records are aircrew.

Royal Air Force operations were recorded on Royal Air Force Forms 540 and 541 in operations record books, and these can be found in a number of different records series according to the status of the unit recording the information.

Squadron operations record books are the most informative; on any given day when flying operations occurred, they tell you when an aircraft took off, the crew, its task and when it landed. If an aircraft was lost, this will also be recorded.

The appendices for units can also tell you about non-flying activities such as promotions, awards, postings to the unit and postings from the unit.

The following records series all contain operations record books:

| | |
|---|---|
| AIR 24 Operations Record Books Commands | Arranged alphabetically |
| AIR 25 Operations Record Books, Groups | Arranged in numerical order by group number |
| AIR 26 Operations Record Books, Wings | Arranged in Wing Number order |
| AIR 27 Operations Record Books, Squadrons | Arranged in order by squadron. The operations record books for the Second World War are available on microfilm |
| AIR 28 Operations Record Books, Royal Air Force Stations | Arranged in alphabetical order by place |
| AIR 29 Operations Record Books, Miscellaneous Units | |

The operations record books in AIR 29 include training units, conversion units, photographic reconnaissance units, Royal Air Force regiment units, air–sea rescue units, and almost every other type of unit completing an operations record book that was not a squadron of the type that would be included in AIR 27.

When aircrew returned from combat operations that included encounters with enemy aircraft they completed a detailed combat report. Combat reports can be found in the series AIR 50 and they are available on microfilm. AIR 50 is arranged according to Command and then in squadron number order.

Planning papers of the various RAF Commands contain much information about the planning and execution of RAF operations; these, together with many reports mentioning units and in some cases personnel, can be found in a number of AIR series, one for each Command. These are as follows:

AIR 13   Balloon Command
AIR 14   Bomber Command
AIR 15   Coastal Command
AIR 16   Fighter Command
AIR 17   Maintenance Command
AIR 23   Overseas Command
AIR 32   Air Training Command
AIR 37   2nd Tactical Air Force
AIR 38   Ferry and Transport Command
AIR 39   Army Co-operation Command.

# THE SOUTH WALES BORDERERS. [ 24 ]

The Sphinx, superscribed "Egypt." **Within a wreath of immortelles the Roman numeral XXIV.**

"**Blenheim**," "**Ramillies**," "**Oudenarde**," "**Malplaquet**," "**Cape of Good Hope, 1806**," "**Talavera**," "**Busaco**," "**Fuentes d'Onor**," "**Salamanca**," "**Vittoria**," "**Pyrenees**," "**Nivelle**," "**Orthes**," "**Peninsula**," "**Chillianwallah**," "**Goojerat**," "**Punjaub**," "**South Africa, 1877-8-9**," "**Burma 1885-87**," "**South Africa, 1900-02**."

*The Great War*—18 *Battalions*.—"**Mons**," "Retreat from Mons," "**Marne 1914**," "Aisne 1914, '18," "Ypres, 1914, '17, '18," "Langemarck, 1914, '17," "**Gheluvelt**," "Nonne Bosschen," "Givenchy, 1914," "Aubers," "Loos," "**Somme 1916, '18**," "Albert, 1916, '18," "Bazentin," "Poziéres," "Flers-Courcelette," "Morval," "Ancre Heights," "Ancre, 1916," "Arras, 1917, '18," "Scarpe, 1917," "Messines, 1917, '18," "Pilckem," "Menin Road," "Polygon Wood," "Broodseinde," "Poelcappelle," "Passchendaele," "**Cambrai**, 1917, '18," "St. Quentin," "Bapaume, 1918," "Lys," "Estaires," "Hazebrouck," "Bailleul," "Kemmel," "Béthune," "Scherpenberg," "Drocourt-Quéant," "Hindenburg Line," "Havrincourt," "Epéhy," "St. Quentin Canal," "Beaurevoir," "Courtrai," "Selle," "Valenciennes," "Sambre," "France and Flanders, 1914-18," "**Doiran, 1917, '18**," "Macedonia, 1915-18," "Helles," "**Landing at Helles**," "Krithia," "Suvla," "Sari Bair," "Scimitar Hill," "Gallipoli, 1915-16," "Egypt, 1916," "Tigris, 1916," "Kut al Amara, 1917," "**Baghdad**," "Mesopotamia, 1916-18," "**Tsingtao**."

*The King's Colours*—A Silver Wreath of Immortelles borne round the Colour pike.

*Agents*—Messrs. Glyn, Mills & Co., Holt's Branch.

*Regimental Journal*—The XXIV Journal of The South Wales Borderers, 10, St. Julian's Avenue, Newport, Mon.

*Regimental Association*—The Regimental Association and Employment Bureau, 10, St. Julian's Avenue Newport, Mon.

Record and Pay Office ... *Exeter.*

## Allied Battalions of Australian Infantry.

18th Battalion (The Kuring-Gai Regiment)
24th Battalion (The Kooyong Regiment)

| | |
|---|---|
| Colonel ... ... ... | Morgan-Owen, Maj.-Gen. Ll. I. G., *C.B., C.M.G., C.B.E., D.S.O.,* ret. pay *(Res. of Off.)* p.s.c†., *(Lt.-Gov. and Sec. R. Hosp. Chelsea)* ... ... ... ... ... ... 30/6/31 |

**Regular Army.**

*Lt.-Colonels.*

§Gottwaltz, P., M.C. (*T/Col.* 15/12/41) 4/5/39
Edwards, J. F., Res. of Off. 24/8 39
Wales, O. M., M.C. (*T/Brig.* 18/5/42) 18/3/41
Cooper, G. C. 4/5/42

*Majors.*

Blackden, C. F. (*T/Lt.-Col.* 18/7/41) (*A/Col.* 21/10/41) (*Empld. K.A.R.*) 3/12/37
Windsor, J. S., M.C. (*T/Lt.-Col.* 15/1/41) 18/8/38
21/12/37
Earle, E. N. G. (*T/Lt.-Col.* 6/9/40) 1/2/38
Napier, V. J. L., M.C., p.s.c†. (*T/Lt.-Col.* 15/10/41) 1/8/38
Popham, V. J. F. (*T/Lt.-Col.* 4/10/40) s. 1/8/38
Tucker, N. R. G. (*Empld. K.A.R.*) 1/8/38
Davies, H. M. (*T/Lt.-Col.* 11/6/42) 1/8/38
Sugden, R. I. (*T/Lt.-Col.* 21/1/41) 26/1/39
Garnons-Williams, J. A. (*T/Lt.-Col.* 23/9/41) spec. emp. 1/2/40
Welch, J. D., p.s.c†. (*T/Lt.-Col.* 30/4/41) 1/2/40
Matthews, F. R. G., p.s.c†. 1/2/40

**Regular Army**—*contd.*

*Majors*—*contd.*

Hope, J. W. (s.c) 30/8/40
Reece, H. M. 30/8/40
Campbell-Miles, D. C., M.B.E. (s.c.) 30/8/40
Jordan, J. L. (*A/Lt.-Col.* 25/5/42) spec. emp. 31/1/41
Reynolds, C. J. 31/1/41
Sugden, G. B., M.B.E. (s.c.) (*T/Lt.-Col.* 27/1/42) s. 30/8/41
Barlow, F. F. S. 30/8/41
de Winton, C. P. G. 29/1/42
Baston, F. W. 25/5/42

*Captains.*

Sewell, E. P., p.s.c. (*W.S./Maj.* 24/9/41) (*T/Lt.-Col.* 24/9/41) s. 27/2/35
Morgan, W. A. (*T/Maj.* 4/2/41) 4/4/35
Martin, A. G., s. 7/8/36
Cox, C. F. (*T/Maj.* 6/5/41) (*A/Lt.-Col.* 27/4/42) 5/8/37
Smyth, K. B. I. (s.c.) [L] (*T/Maj.* 4/12/40) (*A/Lt.-Col.* 22/3/42) s. 5/8/37
Roche, U. E. B. 5/8/37
Rose, C. N. B. (*T/Maj.* 8/12/41) 14/9/37
Galletly, T. H. S., M.C. (*T/Maj.* 14/8/40) (*A/Lt.-Col.* 14/3/42) (*Empld. K.A.R.*) 31/1/38
Home, A. G. D. spec. emp. 18/3/38

**Regular Army**—*contd.*

*Captains*—*contd.*

Stocker, A. J. (s.c.) (*A/Maj.* 15/8/41) 18/3/38.
Cresswell, R. S. (*T/Maj.* 30/5/41) 1/8/38
Moon, I. G. (*T/Maj.* 15/4/41) 1/8/38
Tyler, H. W. (*T/Maj.* 17/9/40) (*Spec. Appt.*) 1/8/38
Crewe-Read, J. O. (s.c.) (*T/Maj.* 4/6/41) s. 1/8/38
Vernon-Harcourt, W. R. D. (*A/Maj.* 24/8/42) (s.c.) 1/8/38
Hamilton, A. C. (s.c.) (*T/Maj.* 14/10/41) s. 1/8/38
Gillespie, R. F. F. (s.c.) (*T/Maj.* 8/3/42) 1/8/38
Rhys, D. L., M.C. (s.c.) 1/8/38
Sheil, F. P. St. M. 1/8/38
Rollin, J. R. (s.c.) (*T/Maj.* 14/11/41) s. 29/1/39
Shipley, C. W. C., Res. of Off. (*T/Maj.* 12/10/41) 24/8/39
Tate, D. D., Res. of Off. 24/8/39
Paterson, M. J. A. (s.c.) (*T/Maj.* 1/4/42) 27/8/39
Yates, D. P. (s.c.) (*T/Maj.* 9/3/41) s. 27/8/39

§Supernumerary.

## Combined Operations

The records of Combined Operations Head-quarters can be found in the series DEFE 2. This series contains a large number of Unit War Diaries for various Commando and Royal Marine commando units and special service battalions.

## SPECIAL OPERATIONS EXECUTIVE

There are two elements to the records of the Special Operations Executive: the personnel records and the records of their activities.

As one might expect, the activities of the Special Operations Executive attract plenty of interest. However unless you know the person you seek was involved with the Special Operations Executive, there is no need to look at those records.

While the records of the Special Operations Executive are fascinating to read, they also contain much that can frustrate a researcher and also much to give food for thought. Reactions can be unpredictable, varying from excitement one minute to tears the next.

## Personnel records

Special Operations Executive personnel records are in the series HS 9 and many of the files are closed under the Data Protection Act. While you may find the name of the individual you are interested in, you may also find that the file is closed. If you can prove that the subject individual is released – usually a copy of the death certificate will suffice – the file will then be opened. HS 9 is listed in alphabetical order, and it is possible to search by name on the Catalogue.

There are other records which concern individuals and these can be found among the operational records.

## Operational records

The operational records of the Special Operations Executive can be found in a number of different records series under the HS prefix, with most of the records arranged by the region in which they took place. There is also a general records series, best approached by keyword searching on the Catalogue. For instance, you can search by opertional code-name since these frequently appear in the records.

HS 1    Far East
HS 2    Scandinavia
HS 3    Africa and Middle East
HS 4    Eastern Europe
HS 5    Balkans
HS 6    Western Europe

## MEDALS, GALLANTRY AND MERITORIOUS SERVICE AWARDS

Medal records for the Second World War period are dominated by recommendations for awards for gallantry or meritorious service. Not only do these recommendations include service personnel, they also include many civilians for their acts of bravery – during the Blitz, for example – as well as their contribution to the war effort.

The other significant series concerning medals relates to the issue of campaign medals awarded to members of the Merchant Navy (see p. 158). The equivalent information for the armed forces is still retained by the Ministry of Defence.

It is very important when looking for information about an award for gallantry or meritorious service to have two items of information: the type of award and when it was announced in *The London Gazette*. There are, of course, many ways to obtain this information but the most effective way is to search *The London Gazette*, either by using the indexes and copies available in the Microfilm Reading Room or by using *The London Gazette* online at *www.gazettes-online.co.uk.*

There are a number of published lists of those granted awards in the Second World War, many of which will tell you when an award was announced in *The London Gazette*. A list of these key published lists can be found in *Medals: The Researcher's Guide* by William Spencer (The National Archives, 2006).

**The Army**

The recommendations for awards granted to members of the British Army, Indian Army and the Australian, Canadian, New Zealand and South African forces can be found in the series WO 373. This is arranged by operational theatre in which the award was won and then in gazette date order. The operational theatre in which an award was won will usually be found at the beginning of the announcement in *The London Gazette*. Apart from all of the obvious operational theatres, recommendations may also be found under the headings 'Non-combat gallantry' (bomb disposal, for example), 'Escape and evasion' and 'Services whilst a POW'.

Many awards announced in *The London Gazette* were announced under the heading of 'Gallant and distinguished service in the field'. Awards announced under this heading can be found in WO 373 under the category of the London Omnibus Collection.

WO 373 is currently being digitized and put on to DocumentsOnline, whereupon it will be possible to search by name, award, operational theatre and unit.

### The Royal Navy and Royal Marines

Recommendations for awards for gallantry and meritorious service for the Royal Navy and Royal Marines can be found in two main series, ADM 1 and ADM 116. Many of the files in these two series are described using operational codenames or specific details about a particular action, such as 'sinking of . . .', 'action against . . .' and then the term 'award(s)'.

It is possible to search for files on the Catalogue using keywords, but by far the most effective method is to use ADM 12 to find the original Admiralty file reference, many of which are prefixed 'H&A', and then converting this into ADM 1 or ADM 116 references. A guide, 'How to Use ADM 12', is available from the Research Enquiries Room. Further information about ADM 12 and how to find files concerning awards for gallantry or meritorious service can be found in *Medals: The Researcher's Guide by William Spencer* (The National Archives, 2006).

### The Royal Air Force

All surviving recommendations for awards granted to Royal Air Force personnel can be found in the series AIR 2. This series also contains recommendations for members of the Royal Australian Air Force, the Royal Canadian Air Force, the Royal New Zealand Air Force and the South African Air Force.

The files contained in AIR 2 may appear to be in no particular order, but they are in fact arranged by a subject code, with code 30 being that for awards.

Many of the files for awards granted in 1943 no longer survive. A name index of the surviving recommendations in AIR 2 has been created and further information can be obtained from Mr Paul Baillie, 14 Wheatfields, St Ives, Huntingdon, Cambs PE17 6YD, tel. 01480 465691.

## Civil Defence

In the Second World War the Civil Defence organization was instituted on a regional basis. While many of the records in HO 186 and HO 207 contain information about Civil Defence policy and activities, without knowing the region in which an incident occurred you will find that researching many aspects of the Civil Defence organization can be very frustrating.

Histories of the Civil Defence organization by region but not including Region 11, Scotland, can be found in HO 186/2950–61.

The majority of Civil Defence records concerning individuals relate to honours and awards.

The Civil Defence organization was split into regions, as follows:

| 1  | Northern       | headquarters Newcastle       |
|----|----------------|------------------------------|
| 2  | North Eastern  | headquarters Leeds           |
| 3  | North Midlands | headquarters Nottingham      |
| 4  | Eastern        | headquarters Cambridge       |
| 5  | London         | headquarters London          |
| 6  | Southern       | headquarters Reading         |
| 7  | South Western  | headquarters Bristol         |
| 8  | Wales          | headquarters Cardiff         |
| 9  | Midlands       | headquarters Birmingham      |
| 10 | North Western  | headquarters Manchester      |
| 11 | Scotland       | headquarters Edinburgh       |
| 12 | South Eastern  | headquarters Tunbridge Wells |

Recommendations for awards granted to civilians involved in the Civil Defence organization, or who were involved in an incident which led to awards being granted, can be found in two different records series.

HO 250 contains the papers of the committee set up to consider recommendations for awards to civilians. This series is arranged by meeting number, with each recommendation discussed at a meeting given a number. There is no name index.

The series T 336 is in many ways similar to the records found in HO 250 but the papers in T 336 are arranged by gazette date. Many of the papers found in this series can also be found in HO 250, but by having the gazette date in the description of each piece in T 336, finding a recommendation for an award may be easier.

A small number of files concerning recommendations for awards can also be found in the series HO 207 Civil Defence Headquarters and Regional Files.

### The Merchant Navy

Many recommendations for awards granted to personnel of the Merchant Navy can be found in the series ADM 1 and ADM 116 (see pp. 153–4).

The main series of records where information concerning awards to Merchant Navy seamen can be found are BT 238, BT 261 and MT 9. Each of these series is either completely or partly concerned with awards. BT 261 contains nothing but awards, whereas BT 238 and MT 9 contain information about other subjects too.

T 335 contains recommendations for awards, and the file description of each piece gives the gazette date upon which the awards were announced.

## Campaign medals

Only the campaign medal records for the Merchant Navy have so far been made available. The equivalent records for the armed forces are still with the Ministry of Defence.

The series BT 395 Database of World War II Medals issued to Merchant Seamen can be searched by name and is available on DocumentsOnline. Each entry in BT 395 provides in tabular form the medal entitlement of an individual. Apart from the name and medal entitlement, BT 395 also provides the date of birth and Discharge A number of an individual, thereby enabling you to find the correct person.

## Long service medals

The only rolls available for long service and good conduct medals are those for the Royal Navy, the Royal Marines, the Royal Naval Reserve and the Royal Naval Volunteer Reserve in ADM 171.

## CASUALTIES

The easiest route to finding out about those who died in the Second World War is to use the Commonwealth War Graves Commission 'Debt of Honour' database at *www.cwgc.org*. Interestingly, civilians who died as a result of enemy action are also listed on the roll of honour. Printed copies of *Civilian War Dead* are available in the library at the National Archives.

A number of archival sources held at the National Archives or the British Library can also provide you with information about casualties, and these include the following.

## The Army

The Army 'Roll of Honour' is available in the series WO 304, and to ease matters it has been turned into a searchable database, available at the National Archives under 'Online and Electronic Resources'. The roll provides place of birth, place of domicile, unit, and place and date of death.

## The Royal Navy and Royal Marines

Listings of naval casualties of the Second World War can be found in the series ADM 104. A published roll of Royal Marine deaths is available in the library.

### The Royal Air Force

There is no single archival source concerning Royal Air Force casualties. Information can be found in a number of different AIR records series, the greatest number of Royal Air Force casualties being in Bomber Command. A number of files concerning Bomber Command casualties can be found in AIR 14.

A number of published sources concerning Royal Air Force casualties are available in the library at the National Archives, including the 'Losses' series published by Midland Publishing.

Casualty record cards for Royal Air Force personnel are held by the Royal Air Force Museum, Hendon.

### The Indian Army

L/MIL/14/143 in the India Office Collection at the British Library lists British casualties of the Indian Army and provides date and cause of death. This casualty list covers 3 September 1939–30 June 1948.

### PRISONERS OF WAR

There are a number of different records series

containing information about prisoners of war. The records take three different forms: record cards, lists of prisoners and personally completed reports. The personally completed reports can be further broken down into two types: escape reports or liberation reports.

WO 344    Liberated Prisoner of War Interrogation Questionnaires. This series is arranged in two alphabetical sequences: prisoners in the hands of the Germans (and formerly the Italians) and prisoners in the hands of the Japanese.

WO 345    Japanese Index Cards of Allied Prisoners of War and Internees, Second World War. Arranged in alphabetical order, these cards provide the date of capture, but please note the year is given as the regnal year of the Emperor Hirohito. Cards of those who died in captivity are crossed through.

WO 392    POW Lists. Printed lists of prisoners held by Germany and its allies during the Second World War. These lists are available on DocumentsOnline or on the open shelves in the library.

WO 208    Directorate of Military Operations and Intelligence, and Directorate of Military Intelligence; Ministry of Defence, Defence

Intelligence Staff: Files. This series contains escape and evasion reports filed by returning personnel who had either avoided capture or escaped from a prisoner-of-war camp. WO 208/3298–327 cover events prior to D Day and WO 208/3348–52 cover events post D Day. There are nominal indexes available in the Research Enquiries Room. These records include all three armed services and the Merchant Navy.

AIR 40      This series contains a small number of reports, completed by Royal Air Force aircrew who had been shot down and returned to the UK, in AIR 40/2072–3, AIR 40/1533 and 1545–52.

An alphabetical list of all Royal Air Force and Dominion aircrew held by the Germans in 1944–5 can be found in AIR 20/2336.

The Indian Army Prisoner of War Card Index is available at the British Library.

## COURTS MARTIAL

Naval courts martial records are in the series ADM 156 and ADM 178, and it is possible to search the Catalogue by name of the individual who was tried.

Army courts martial charge books up to 1948 are in the series WO 84.

The records of Army courts martial are spread over a number of different records series. Proceedings of courts martial are in the series WO 71 and the Catalogue can be searched by the name of the accused.

Registers of Army Field General Courts Martial and Military Courts are in the series WO 213. The information in this series is arranged by the date the information was received by the Judge Advocate General and is in the form of a one-line entry giving service details, date of trial, offence and sentence.

Registers of District Courts Martial at Home (H) and Abroad (A) can be found in WO 86 (H&A), WO 90 (A) and WO 92 (H).

The Royal Air Force courts martial records can be found in AIR 18 Proceedings, AIR 21 Register of Courts Martial and AIR 43 Charge Books.

## THE MERCHANT NAVY

The records of the Merchant Navy for the Second World War cover a vast array of record types. There are records of service, ships' logs, ship movement records and a roll of

1. No. *1579149*　　RANK *SST.*　　SURNAME *KEELING*

　CHRISTIAN NAMES *CHARLES TREVOR*

2. LECTURES before Capture :

　(a) Were you lectured in your unit on how to behave in the event of capture?
　　(State where, when and by whom).

　　　*YES  SANDTOFT. H.CON UNIT.*

　(b) Were you lectured on escape and evasion?　(State where, when and by whom).

　　　*YES  SANDTOFT. H.CON UNIT.*

3. INTERROGATION after capture :

　Were you specially interrogated by the enemy?　(State where, when and methods employed by enemy).

　　　*YES.  OBERURSAL (FRANKFURT). 18/8/44. THREATENED OS*

　　*SPY AND SHOOTING.*

4. ESCAPES attempted :

　Did you make any attempted or partly successful escapes?　(Give details of each attempt separately, stating where,
　when, method employed, names of your companions, where and when recaptured and by whom.　Were you
　physically fit?　What happened to your companions?)

　　　*NO*

5. SABOTAGE :

　Did you do any sabotage or destruction of enemy factory plant, war material, communications, etc., when employed
　on working-parties or during escape?　(Give details, places and dates.)

　　　*NO*

6. COLLABORATION with enemy :

　Do you know of any British or American personnel who collaborated with the enemy or in any way helped the
　enemy against other Allied Prisoners of War?　(Give details, names of person(s) concerned, camp(s), dates
　and nature of collaboration or help given to enemy).

　　　*NO.*

7. WAR CRIMES :

　If you have any information or evidence of bad treatment by the enemy to yourself or to others, or knowledge of
　any enemy violation of Geneva Convention you should ask for a copy of " Form Q " on which to make your
　statement.

　(NOTE : Form Q is a separate form inviting information on " War Crimes" and describe the treatment.)

honour. The following records series will all help in your pursuit of a member of the Merchant Navy serving between 1939 and 1945.

BT 372    Central Register of Seamen: Seamen's Records ('Pouches') 1913–2002. Each pouch is identified by name, Discharge A number, place and date of birth.

BT 382    Fifth Register of Merchant Seaman's Service (CRS 10 forms) 1941–72. These are arranged in ranges of names. There may be more than one reference covering the name.

BT 391    Special Operations Records, COMNO Pouches. These seamen's pouches are from the Combined Office Merchant Navy Operations and are arranged in alphabetical order. They can be searched by name on the Catalogue and provide Discharge A number and date and place of birth. These records primarily concern those merchant seamen involved in the liberation of Europe.

BT 380    Primarily Second World War: Log Books, Crew Agreements and Associated Records. The logs are arranged on a yearly basis and by ship's official number.

BT 381        Coast Trade Ships Official Log Books and Crew Agreements 1939 to 1945. These logs are arranged on a yearly basis and by ship's official number.

BT 387        Second World War Log Books and Agreements and Crew Lists of Allied Foreign Ships, Requisitioned or Chartered by His Majesty's Government. These are arranged in alphabetical ranges by name of ship.

BT 389        Second World War, Merchant Shipping Movement Cards. These cards are arranged in two alphabetical sequences.

BT 390        Merchant Seamen who Served on Royal Navy Ships under the T124X and T124T Agreements: T124X and T124T Pouches. These pouches are arranged by name, and it is possible to search by name on the Catalogue. Each entry also provides Discharge A number and place and date of birth.

BT 339        Rolls of Honour, Wars of 1914–18 and 1939–45

## THE HOME FRONT

Although people in Britain were subjected to air raids in the latter part of the First World

War, it was in the Second World War that all of the population were affected by the threat of aerial attack. The carrying of gas masks became compulsory; evacuation of children from those areas considered at greatest threat from air attack took place, with many children being sent overseas, not just to other parts of the UK.

The whole population was involved in the war effort and many people were employed by the state in areas of duty other than in the armed forces. The Women's Land Army, the Auxiliary and later National Fire Service and the Civil Defence organization all fall into this category, and the records relating to some of their activities can be found among the records at the National Archives.

### The Home Guard

Records concerning the Home Guard contain very little concerning individuals.

At the time of writing, the records of service of men who served in the Home Guard (Army Form W3066) are still retained by the Ministry of Defence. Until such time as they are released, there are very few sources available in the

National Archives concerning the Home Guard.

There are a number of recommendations for awards, most notably in AIR 2/9040 which contains details of a large number of British Empire Medals awarded to members of the Home Guard on stand-down in late 1944. Other recommendations for awards may be found in WO 373.

Home Guard records of service are held on behalf of the Ministry of Defence by TNT Archive Service, Tetron Point, William Nadin Way, Swadlincote, Derbyshire, DE11 0BB, tel: 01283 227 911/912/913, fax: 01283 227 942. Limited information is available to either those who served or their next of kin.

Officers commissioned into the Home Guard are listed in the *Home Guard List*, copies of which can be found in the Microfilm Reading Room. Each list is arranged by command with a name index at the back of each section. An entry will tell you the specific Home Guard unit in which an individual served, which can be useful when looking for a unit history. Home Guard commissions were announced in Home Guard Orders and not *The London Gazette*.

A number of Home Guard histories, many produced at the end of the war, can be found in the series WO 199. The best way to find these is to search the Catalogue by unit name. A list of these histories can be found in *Militia and Volunteer Forces 1757–1945* by William Spencer (Public Record Office, 1997).

One aspect of Home Guard history still remains fairly secret, and that is the auxiliary units. Nominal rolls of some of these units can be found in WO 199.

### The Women's Land Army

The index records of service (only the index surviving) of members of the Women's Land Army are in the series MAF 421 and are arranged in alphabetical order on microfiche.

### Conscientious objectors

Under the National Service (Armed Forces) Act of 1940, men between the ages of 18 and 41 were liable for military service. As had happened in the First World War, many individuals registered as conscientious objectors.

An incomplete series of registers of those who were registered as conscientious objectors

**The *Home Guard List***
Produced between September 1941 and October 1944, the *Home Guard List* records all officers of the Home Guard. Each List is arranged by geographical region and is name indexed.

The *Home Guard List* was arranged into the regions:

Anti-Aircraft Command (October 1944 only)
Eastern Command
London District
Northern Command
Scottish Command
Southern Command
South Eastern Command
Western Command.

An officer's entry will tell you their rank, when the commission at that rank was announced in Home Guard Orders, and the unit in which they served. The unit details can be very informative as they usually mention the place for which the particular unit was responsible. By using the unit information from the *Home Guard List* and applying it to the Catalogue, it is possible to establish whether a unit history survives in WO 199.

can be found in the series LAB 45. The registers are in no particular order and start in 1939; they can be found in LAB 45/75, 76 and 84.

Samples of other documents relating to

conscientious objectors can be found in LAB 45/51–60. Other examples for those registered in the Midland region can be found in LAB 45/162–4.

*Further reading*
THE ROYAL NAVY AND ROYAL MARINES
Bruno Pappalardo, *Tracing Your Naval Ancestors* (Public Record Office, 2003)

THE ROYAL AIR FORCE
C.G. Jefford, *RAF Squadrons* (Airlifo, 1000)
William Spencer, *Air Force Records. A Guide for Family Historians* (The National Archives, 2008)

MEDALS
William Spencer, *Medals: The Researcher's Guide* (The National Archives, 2006)

THE MERCHANT NAVY
K. Smith, C.T. Watts and M.J. Watts, *Records of Merchant Shipping and Seamen* (Public Record Office, 1998)

Chapter 4

# Post-war: 1945–53

- Records of service
- Military operations after August 1945
  *Army operational records*
  *Royal Navy and Royal Air Force*
  *operational records*
- Key theatres of operation post-1945
  *Palestine*
  *Malaya*
  *Korea*
  *Prisoners of war (Korean War)*
  *Kenya*
  *Other operations*
- Courts martial
- Medals

## SETTING THE SCENE

Many post-Second World War operations are covered by the records mentioned in this section. After 1945 the British armed forces conducted operations in Palestine, South East Asia, Malaya, Korea and Kenya. A new aspect of British Army soldiering was the garrisoning of West Germany, something that continues to this day.

A large number of the men involved in the operations whose records are discussed in this section were National Servicemen rather than regulars.

Many of the series of operational records discussed in this chapter have already been mentioned but, as with the earlier periods, many new records series will also need to be consulted.

## RECORDS OF SERVICE

Apart from the records of the Merchant Navy, all of which have been discussed in previous sections, there are no military records of service available for this period as they are all still with the Ministry of Defence. A contact address for the Ministry of Defence can be found on p. 232.

**The *Air Force List***

The first *Air Force List* was published in April 1918. As one might expect, arrangement of the *List* varies over the period under discussion. The name index of the early editions provides a page number for an individual, and the entry on a page will give you the rank, seniority and specialization. The specialization is usually abbreviated and there is a key in the *List*.

For the period between the two world wars, the *Air Force List* will tell you which specific unit the individual was serving in, and in what capacity. From September 1939 onwards the index of the *Air Force List* gives the officer's personal number as well as the usual page number.

The *Air Force List* includes officers of the Auxiliary Air Force and the Royal Air Force Volunteer Reserve as each of the services was created.

Retired Royal Air Force officers can be found in the January or Spring editions of the *Air Force List* from c.1945 onwards, and each entry will provide you with date of birth, date of first commission, final rank and the date appointed to that rank, and retirement date.

Some information about officers of the armed forces can be found in the *Army List, Navy List* and *Air Force List*.

## MILITARY OPERATIONS AFTER AUGUST 1945

### Army operational records

Operational records in the immediate period after the Second World War and up to the end of 1946 can be found in the Unit War Diary series in the range WO 166–77, as mentioned in Chapter 3.

After 1946 unit operational records are called Quarterly Historical Reports and can chiefly be found in the following series:

| | |
|---|---|
| British Army of the Rhine | WO 267 |
| British Element Trieste Force | WO 264 |
| British Troops Austria | WO 263 |
| Caribbean | WO 270 |
| Central Mediterranean Forces | WO 262 |
| East and West Africa | WO 269 |
| Far East | WO 268 |
| Gibraltar | WO 266 |
| Home Forces | WO 271 |
| Malta | WO 265 |
| Middle East (including Palestine) | WO 261 |

After 1950, Quarterly Historical Reports were replaced by Unit Historical Records, and these are in the series WO 305. It is possible to locate a reference for WO 305 by using the Catalogue.

Unlike the Second World War diaries, personnel are not mentioned frequently and returns of officers are not common, especially in WO 305.

Apart from the records mentioned above, the following records are collected together under the appropriate operational theatre headings. These records are in many cases specific to that operational theatre.

**Royal Navy and Royal Air Force operational records**

Operational records for ships of the Royal Navy and squadrons of the Royal Air Force can still be found in series ADM 53 and AIR 27 respectively. Submarine logs can be found in the series ADM 173. References in these series can be pinpointed by using the Catalogue and by searching by ship's name or squadron number and the year of interest.

## KEY THEATRES OF OPERATION POST-1945

### Palestine, 27 September 1945–30 June 1948

| | |
|---|---|
| ADM 53 | Ships' Logs |
| ADM 173 | Submarine Logs |
| AIR 27 | Squadron Operations Record Books |
| WO 261 | Middle East Land Forces: Quarterly Historical Reports |

| Distance run through the Water / Zone Time kept at noon −1 | Position | | Latitude N | Longitude E | Depending on | Currents experienced | Number on Sick List | ANCHOR BEARINGS |
|---|---|---|---|---|---|---|---|---|
| | 0800 | | 71  42 | 15  57 | DR | | 6 | |
| | 1200 | | 72  07 | 20  48 | Obs'd | | | |
| | 2000 | | 72  30 | 28  15 | D.R. | | | |
| | | 1ᵃ ⁶ˢ | 080 250 | | | | | 1445  Jamaica stationed astern |
| 1300 10661 | 14  2 | | 060  161·9 | | | | | 1401  26 knots  1412  24 knots  1453  Eng 7 |
| 1400 1089·1 | 24  — | | 060  192 | | | | | Km ⁵ 360°  1507 ¾ 050  1523 ¾ 080 |
| | 21  9 | | 060 | | | | | 1537 ¾ 050°  1557 ¾ 080 |
| 1500 1112·4 | 2  4 | | 360  195·6 | | | | | 1614 ¾ 090° |
| | | | 360 080 080 080 | | | | | 1617  Radar surface contact single sole |
| 1600 1135·6 | 6  9 6  4 | | 090 090  192 | WSW 7 5 | 47 99 68 41 39 44 | | | 020  45.000°  1630 ¾ 070  1635 ¾ |
| 1700 | 12  5 | | Var  1978 | | | | | 060  1644 ¾ 080  27 knots |
| | | | | | | | | 1650  Enemy Battlecruiser sighted + engaged |
| | | | | | | | | wit main + secondary armament at 12000° |
| | | | | | | | | Believed to be "Scharnhorst". Enemy |
| | | | | | | | | turned to Port. The Norfolk had now |
| 1800 | 26  9 | | Var  2283 | | | | | engaged by British Cruisers + the had |
| 1900 | 26  9 | | Var  229·1 | | | | | Eastward.  Battle became a chase to the |
| | | | | | | | | Eastward.  wit "Duke of York" Keeping west + |
| 2000 | 25  — | | Var  204·1 | | | | | west of the convoy.  Cannon various runs toward. |
| | 9  4 | | Var | | | | | 1824  Cheers fire  range  22000° |
| 2100 1255·4 | 12  5 | | 090  1527 | | | | | 1850  Target struck on convoy by 2 salvoes |
| | | | | | | | | of Pentagon  1901  Reopened fire at convoy |
| 2200 1276·1 | 27  — | | 090  192·6 | | | | | wit main armament at 7000°  1929 |
| | | | | | | | | Cheers fire  range  4000°  Convoy + Battleship |
| 2300 1299·1 | 18  8 6  2 | | 090 120  205 | | | | | out in the finish off the convoy wit the Topedo |
| | | | | | | | | 1945  German Battlecruiser "Scharnhorst" sank |

| WO 275 | Sixth Airborne Division, Palestine: Papers and Reports |

## Malaya, 16 June 1948–31 July 1960

| ADM 53 | Ships' Logs |
| ADM 173 | Submarine Logs |
| AIR 27 | Squadron Operations Record Books |
| WO 268 | Far East Land Forces: Quarterly Historical Reports |
| WO 305 | Army Unit Historical Records and Reports |

## Korea, 2 July 1950–27 July 1953

| ADM 53 | Ships' Logs |
| ADM 173 | Submarine Logs |
| ADM 202 | Royal Marine Unit Records |
| AIR 27 | Squadron Operations Record Books |
| WO 281 | British Commonwealth Division of United Nations Force: War Diaries, Korean War |
| WO 308 | Historical Records and Reports: Korean War |

## Prisoners of war (Korean War)

Records concerning prisoners held by Korea can be found in a number of different records series. A list of British and Commonwealth prisoners between January 1951 and July 1953 can be found in WO 208/3999. A further list of prisoners of war compiled in January 1954 is in

WO 308/54. Other correspondence about prisoners of war can be found in WO 32/19273, WO 162/208–64 and DO 35/5853–63.

The records in WO 162/208–64 are arranged by name of the person who completed the report. These reports were used to find out about any other prisoners the compiler may have seen or had information about.

### Kenya, 21 October 1952–17 November 1956

Although the operations in Kenya during the Mau Mau uprising ended after 1953, they do fall within the chronological range of this book. Many of the service personnel who took part in the operations in Kenya had previously seen service in Korea and Malaya.

| | |
|---|---|
| ADM 53 | Ships' Logs |
| ADM 173 | Submarine Logs |
| AIR 27 | Squadron Operations Record Books |
| WO 276 | East African Command Papers |
| WO 305 | Unit Historical Records |

### Other operations

It is possible to find records for other well-known post-Second World War activities such as the Berlin Air Lift and the Yangtse Incident.

Records concerning the Berlin Air Lift (Operation Plainfare) can be found in a number of different AIR series including AIR 2, AIR 8, AIR 10 and AIR 20/6891–4.

The Yangtse Incident involved HMS *Amethyst*, which was detained on the Yangtse River, and HMS *Black Swan*, HMS *Consort* and HMS *London*. Apart from log books in ADM 53, various reports and files concerning the incident can be found in ADM 1 and ADM 116, including the final report in ADM 110/5740, 5740A and 5740B.

## COURTS MARTIAL

Naval courts martial records are in the series ADM 156 and ADM 178; it is possible to search the Catalogue by name of the individual tried.

Army courts martial charge books up to 1948 are in the series WO 84.

The records of Army courts martial are spread over a number of different records series. Proceedings of courts martial are in the series WO 71 and the Catalogue can be searched by the name of the accused.

Registers of Army Field General Courts Martial and Military Courts are in the series

WO 213. The information in this series is arranged by the date the information was received by the Judge Advocate General and is in the form of a one-line entry giving service details, date of trial, offence and sentence.

Register of District Courts Martial at Home (H) and Abroad (A) can be found in WO 86 (H&A), WO 90 (A) and WO 92 (H).

The Royal Air Force courts martial records can be found in AIR 18 Proceedings, AIR 21 Register of Courts Martial and AIR 43 Charge Books.

## MEDALS

There are very few post-Second World War medal records available. At the time of writing a small number of medal rolls for the Army are being transferred, and these include rolls for the General Service Medal with clasps South East Asia 1945–6, Palestine 1945–8 and Bomb and Mine Clearance. When available they will be in the series WO 100.

The medal roll for the 1953 Coronation Medal is available on the open shelves in the Library. The roll is arranged in alphabetical order.

Recommendations for awards for gallantry

and meritorious service are in records series already mentioned. Files for awards to the Royal Navy and Royal Marines can be found in ADM 1 and ADM 116; Royal Air Force recommendations are in the series AIR 2, and those for the Army in WO 373. Example of files for the Royal Air Force include AIR 2/9986 for awards for the Berlin Air Lift, AIR 2/16814 for awards for Malaya and AIR 2/16815 for awards for Korea.

Included in WO 373 are recommendations for awards for all operations since the Second World War up to 1991, except those for Northern Ireland. As before, WO 373 is arranged by operational theatre and then by gazette date. Also in WO 373 are recommendations for non-combat gallantry and New Year and Birthday Honours Lists.

**APPEAL DECISION**

REFUGEE—FEMALE

(1) Surname (*block capitals*) ... EISNER

    Forenames ... Marie

    Alias ...

(2) Date and place of birth ... 12th April 1899 : Vienna.

(3) Nationality ... German by annexation.

(4) Police Regn. Cert. No. ... 571670     Home Office reference, if known ...

        Special Procedure Card Number, if known ...

(5) Address ... Glanville, Minehead, Somerset.

(6) Normal occupation ... Secretary to Film Company.

(7) Present Occupation ... Domestic servant

(8) Decision of Tribunal   ~~Left subject to 6A & 9A~~  }   Strike out which do not apply.
       ~~Left subject to 9A~~
       Exempt from 6A & 9A

(9) Decision of Advisory Committee   Exempted from 6A & 9A  }   Strike out which does not apply.
       ~~Left subject to 6A & 9A~~

*53m (6 sorts) 3/40—[8338] 10050/667 30m 4/40 4070 G & S 704

[OVER

## Reasons for Decision.

This woman is a Jewess and is unmarried. She was dep[rived]
of her employment as a secretary to a film company for
reasons and came to England on the 12th. November 1938

Her parents are dead.

The woman is of superior type and is now working as a
for Miss Allen, "Glanville", Minehead, who attended as
referee, and spoke well of EISNER.

After interviewing the alien, the Advisory Committee f[elt]
the opinion that she is a genuine racial refugee, and
her being at liberty constitutes no danger to the Stat[e]

[Region]al Advisory Committee ... No. 7. BRISTOL.

[Signat]ure *Richard O'Sullivan*

Date ... 13th. July 1[9...]

Chapter 5

# Consequences of war

- Leaving and returning home
  *Records*
- Changed lives
  *Aliens and internees*
  *Refugees*
  *Evacuees*

## SETTING THE SCENE

During times of war the state keeps information about those individuals who are affected by the war and also those who may have an affect on the war. For instance, during the war refugees were taken in by Britain while at the same time the country had to deal with enemy aliens already living here. Both these groups of people may also have been spies and have had an affect on the war in this capacity.

Other groups of people affected by the war were those Allied personnel who came to serve here, who married British nationals and who left these shores with their new spouses after the war had ended. Some Allied servicemen left behind offspring of whom they had no knowledge.

## LEAVING AND RETURNING HOME

In the days before air travel, the way most service personnel and their families travelled around the world was by ship, as did those people who left Britain after the two world wars for new lives overseas.

There are a number of aspects to researching those leaving or returning to Britain that need to be considered. Was the individual a service person? Where were they going? When did they travel?

## Records

WO 25 | There are numerous 'Embarkation' and 'Disembarkation' records in this series. Many go up to the outbreak of the Second World War. However, unless the individual was an officer, then names are rarely mentioned. The majority of the information is statistical. Where families are mentioned, the record usually says 'wife and children (by number) of' and the officer's name only. The address the individuals are travelling to or from may sometimes be mentioned, especially between the wars.

The most informative records concerning leaving, re-entering or entering the United Kingdom are the records created by the Board of Trade. There are two series:

BT 26 | Inwards Passenger Lists 1878–1960. These are arranged on a yearly basis and then in alphabetical order by port of arrival. Unless you know the port of arrival, name of ship and the date, any search will be lengthy.

BT 27        Outwards Passenger Lists 1890–1960.
             These records are arranged chronologically
             and in alphabetical order by port of
             departure. These records are currently
             being digitized and are being made available
             at *www.ancestorsonboard.com*, where it is
             possible to search by name. For further
             information about what is currently available,
             see the website.

Many people leaving the United Kingdom after the Second World War were servicemen from other countries such as the United States of America and Canada. A large number of these individuals left behind children or expectant mothers and returned to their place of origin. Tracking down these fathers has been for many a lifelong task. A very useful website for researching American service personnel can be found at *www.gitrace.org*.

Very few British records help in such searches, but help in the form of a gazetteer stating which American unit was where, and when, is available on CD-ROM at the National Archives.

## CHANGED LIVES

Wars are not solely about the service person-nel who took part or the civilians who contributed to the war effort. Many people's lives were changed, restricted or altered for ever just because they were, in many cases, in the wrong place at the wrong time. Aliens, internees, refugees and evacuees all fall into this category and they are very much part of the records kept by the state, especially during the two world wars.

## Aliens and internees

Lists of Germans interned in the First World War can be found in WO 900/45 and 46. A further list of those exempt from internment in 1915 and a list of internees for 1918 can be found in HO 144/11720.

A census of aliens from 1915 to 1924, including male enemy aliens of the age of 45 and upwards, can be found in HO 45/11522/287235.

Records concerning internees and aliens for the Second World War can be found in three key Home Office records series. A sample of 75 personal files can be found in HO 214. In HO 215 can be found nominal lists of internees and the lists record date of birth and date of release. HO 215 is arranged by name of internment camp.

HO 396, which is available on microfilm, contains sets of index cards for enemy aliens from Germany, Austria and Italy. The sets consist of those considered for internment but who were at liberty, and those who were actually interned. Most cards contain biographical information, address, occupation and employer's details where appropriate. There are also a number of other lists of internees, both male and female, German, Italian and Austrian.

The key sections of HO 396 are arranged as follows;

| | |
|---|---|
| HO 396/1–106 | Internees at Liberty, A–Z |
| HO 396/107–14 | Internees Interned in Canada, A–Z |
| HO 396/119–24 | Non-resident Seamen Interned in Canada, A–Z |
| HO 396/139–45 | Internees Interned in Australia, A–Z |
| HO 396/165–204 | German Internees Released in the United Kingdom, A–Z |
| HO 396/205–12 | Italian Internees Released in the United Kingdom, A–Z |
| HO 396/214–43 | Index of Wives of Dead Germans, A–Z |
| HO 396/245–83 | Germans Interned in the United Kingdom in 1939, A–Z |
| HO 396/284–94 | Italians Interned in the United Kingdom in 1939, A–Z |

Samples of aliens' record cards kept by the Metropolitan Police are in the series MEPO 35. These cards record the full name, date of birth, date of arrival in the United Kingdom, employment history, address, marital status and if the individual had any children. If the subject individual was later naturalized, the Home Office details would be recorded on the card. Most cards contain a photograph of the individual.

### Refugees

Record cards for refugees from Belgium in the First World War can be found in the series MH 8. These cards are arranged in alphabetical order and are in MH 8/39–93

Records of the Czechoslovak Refugee Trust are in the series HO 294 where specimen case files for refugee families can be found in HO 294/235–486. Other case papers can be found in HO 294/487–611.

### Evacuees

Although thousands of children were evacuated from major cities to places of safety in the country, very few files about individuals are held by the National Archives, the majority being policy files about how the evacuation was to be conducted. Files concerning individual schools can be found in ED 32.

A large number of children were evacuated overseas. The records of the Children's Overseas Reception Board can be found in the series DO 131, where a number of case files can be found in DO 131/106–12. The catalogue descriptions for these pieces of DO 131 are currently being improved. Work to extract the names of all children mentioned in each file will eventually mean that it will be possible to identify each child who travelled overseas under this scheme and will enable researchers to search by name of individual. The files concerning a number of women who escorted the children to their destination can be found in DO 131/71–87. Other records in DO 131 include registers of child applicants for the scheme and unregistered lists of children considered by the Children's Overseas Reception Board. The London County Council record of the evacuation can be seen in ED 138/48.

Perhaps one of the most significant incidents regarding child evacuees was the sinking of the *City of Benares* on 17 September 1940. The case files of five children who survived the sinking can be found in DO 131/88–92. Other files concerning the loss of the vessel can be found in HO 186 and MT 9 by keyword-searching the Catalogue.

A large number of records that concern evacuees can be found amongst the records of the India Office held by the British Library.

Evacuee Registers of those who fled from Burma after the Japanese invasion can be found in M/8/57–58. Records in L/PJ/8381–150 concern refugees and evacuees in Indian camps and in many cases there are nominal rolls of those held in such camps. Similar records can also be found in L/AG/40/1.

India Office records concerning internees for the Second World War period can be found in L/PJ/8/30–76 and nominal rolls are included in these records.

For further information see *Family History on the Move* (The National Archives, 2006) and *Immigrants and Aliens* (The National Archives, 2004), both by R. Kershaw and M. Pearsall.

| Place | Date | Hour | Summary of Events and information | References to Appendices |
|---|---|---|---|---|
| CHUNGGJAN | 4th Nov | 1720 hrs | Pls at CT 176224 and D Coy on Pt 217 being attacked. | |
| | | 1740 hrs | B Coy being attacked. | |
| | | 1805 hrs | C Coy withdrew. Men collected at MMG HQ CT 198198. | |
| | | 1820 hrs | En penetrate wire defences round Pt 217. | |
| | | 1850 hrs | B Coy posn overrun. B Coy Comd ordered to withdraw to Battle Patrol posn CT 175216. Pl on Pt 217 overrun and out of touch with Coy HQ. | |
| | | 1915 hrs | D Coy ordered to reinforce Pt 217 with pl from CT 182216 | |
| | | 2045 hrs | 3" Mors ordered to withdraw to CT 195203 after firing off maximum amount of ammunition. Confirmed B Coy in posn CT 175216. | |
| | | 2050 hrs | Battle Patrol and elements of B Coy withdraw to pl of A Coy at CT 178208. | |
| | | 2115 hrs | 3" Mors at new posn CT 195203. Pl of C Coy and pl of D Coy still holding on CT 176224. B Coy and Battle Patrol in posn with A Coy pl CT 178209 | |
| | | 2355 hrs | OC D Coy now in posn CT 182216 with one complete pl and remains of pl and Coy HQ from Pt 217. | Not discovered until 0820 x hrs 5 Nov 51. |
| | 5th Nov | 0203 hrs | Confirmed that pl of C Coy and pl of D Coy still holding at CT 176224 and orders sent for the group to withdraw, C Coy pl to go to the Bn HQ area, D Coy pl to go to CTVA182216. | Not confirmed until 0127 hrs 5 Nov 51. |
| | | 0340 hrs | D Coy pl from CT 176224 now in posn with remainder of D Coy CT 182216. Coy posns now:- | |
| | | | A Coy pl CT 173209 | |
| | | | pl CT 183209 | |
| | | | pl CT 188211 | |
| | | | B Coy CT 178209 | |
| | | | C Coy CT 195198 | |
| | | | D Coy x CT 182216 | |
| | | | Battle Patrol CT 185206 | |
| | | | Main HQ CT 182199 | |

Chapter 6

# Research advice

- Techniques and tips
  *Officers*
  *Soldiers*
  *Sailors*
  *Operational records*
  *Civilians employed in the armed forces*
  *Online searching*
  *The London Gazette online*
  *Using the National Archives' Catalogue*
  *Cases to make you think*

- Quick references
  *Records of service*
  *Operations (key series)*
  *Army order of preference*
  *Ranks*

## TECHNIQUES AND TIPS

Everyone likes to research in their own particular way, and if the records are available the results of their research are dictated by the techniques they use. With the advent of digitization of records, computerization of catalogues and ever-changing terminology, be it for example an abbreviation or unit title, finding records requires a flexible approach but also, in many cases, specific knowledge. Using the correct approach for specific types of records can usually yield better results than a lucky stab in the dark or a name search. The following techniques may be helpful in providing an approach to research.

### Officers

The first thing to do when researching an officer is to find him or her in the appropriate *List*: the *Navy List* for officers of the naval forces and Royal Marines, the *Army List* for all officers of the Army or the *Air Force List* for officers of the Royal Air Force. This might seem obvious or simplistic, but the *Lists* contain a lot of information that has to be used when looking at archival sources. The appropriate *List* will tell you when the officer was commissioned and the rank held at the time of publication. Unit details and awards in the form of post-nominal letters all appear in the *Lists*. Most *Lists* contain casualty lists and the date of death of an individual.

Unlike the *Army* and *Air Force Lists*, which usually have just one alphabetical index, the *Navy List* has a separate name index for the Royal Navy, the Royal Naval Reserve and one for the Royal Naval Volunteer Reserve too, so it is important to check them all if you are unsure of which part of the naval services an officer was in.

In the 20th century, the records of a naval officer may be in two or more different places in ADM 196. Once an officer reached the rank of Captain a separate record of his confidential reports was kept in another piece of ADM 196. These confidential reports are arranged by date from when the officer reached the rank of Captain, a date which can be ascertained by using the *Navy List*.

During the First World War officers who ended up serving in the Royal Air Force may have come from one of three places:

1 Officers could have been in any other part of the Army, transferred into the Royal Flying Corps and then into the Royal Air Force.

2 Naval officers from the Royal Naval Air Service could elect to transfer to the Royal Air Force upon its creation or return to naval service.

3 The final route into the Royal Air Force was by direct entry after 1 April 1918.

Taking the three routes into account, the following sources may need to be consulted:

1 WO 339/WO 374 then AIR 76;
2 ADM 196/ADM 273 then AIR 76;
3 AIR 76 only.

As an example of how an officer can appear in several records, my grandfather's brother joined the Royal Naval Air Service as a rating and is found in ADM 188. Commissioned into the Royal Naval Air Service, he is also found in ADM 273. He transferred out of the Royal Naval Air Service into the Royal Naval Volunteer Reserve and is in ADM 337. Finally he ended as an armaments officer in the Royal Air Force and is in AIR 76!

If there is no record of service available for an officer, all is not lost. Gathering information from a variety of sources such as the *Navy, Army or Air Force List, The London Gazette*, medal and operational records will give you almost everything but basic biographical and medical information.

### Soldiers

Researching a soldier who served at any time between 1899 and 1918 is fraught with potential failure, solely because of the fact that so many records of service were destroyed by enemy action in 1940.

The terms and conditions of enlistment for soldiers between 1899 and 1920 varied immensely and were subject to change according to the needs of the Army. During the First World War many men enlisted for 'the duration of the war', which with hindsight was a very brave thing to do when no one knew how long it was going to last!

Pre-war Territorial Force soldiers whose terms of engagement expired between 1914 and 1916 were given the option of signing on for further service, and many who did so were given a long period of leave between the end of their old engagement and the beginning of their next one. As for those Territorial Force soldiers who did not commit themselves for further service and who returned home, they became subject to the laws of conscription and ended up back in the Army anyway.

With the advent of digitized First World War soldiers' records on *www.ancestry.co.uk*, when this project is completed it will be possible to search for an individual record of service by name, number or unit. However, there can be problems when searching for individuals online and in digitized records in particular. Incorrect transcription of records can lead to many errors and many frustrated searches. This is especially galling when you know the information you are seeking is there.

In the First World War, most officers commissioned after 1915 came from the ranks and your officer's record of service, should you locate it in WO 339 or WO 339, may contain his other-rank papers.

Searching the series WO 97 for the papers of many of the soldiers who were discharged between 1899 and 1913 can result in failure.

There are many reasons for this, but it is always worth looking in the First World War papers.

If a man had left the Army between 1899 and 1913 and rejoined, he was obliged to declare his former service. Once the Army knew a man had seen previous service, it would usually ask the regimental or corps record office for his old papers. As with so many, the majority of papers for men discharged between 1914 and 1920 were destroyed in 1940. The records of men who had seen service many years before the First World War, and in the First World War as well, were among those destroyed.

Many old and bold soldiers who were senior non-commissioned officers in the late 19th and early 20th centuries, and who left the Army prior to 1914, returned to the colours and were commissioned between 1914 and 1918. Many did not see service overseas, but if they did it should be possible to find them in the Medal Index Cards.

### Sailors

Royal Naval ratings fall into three distinct

**Remember Henry Webber**

Many people researching soldiers who saw service in the late 19th century often fail to find them where they expect, in WO 97. There are always a number of possible reasons why a man is missing from the papers in WO 97 but here is something to make you think.

Researcher: 'I can't find my man in WO 97. I know he was in the Army in 1897 but I have looked in WO 97 for men discharged between 1883 and 1900, and 1900 and 1913 and he's not there.'

Advisor: 'How old was he in 1914?'

Researcher: 'Thirty-five.'

Advisor: 'When conscription came in during the First World War, the maximum age that a man could be called up, depending upon circumstances, was 55. Prior to conscription, there was no reason to stop a man from volunteering for the Army. A man called Henry Webber volunteered for the Army and he was commissioned as an officer. Henry Webber is the oldest known operational casualty of the First World War – he was 68 when he died in 1916!'

If you can't find an old soldier from the late 19th century, try looking in the First World War records in WO 363 and WO 364. You may also try PIN 26. A Rorke's Drift VC winner is in PIN 26, and he saw service in the First World War.

categories: Royal Navy, Royal Naval Reserve and Royal Naval Volunteer Reserve. It is therefore very important to know the service number of a naval rating as this will indicate which of the three categories the individual comes from.

For records dating from during the First World War there is a dangerous red herring in the form of service numbers prefixed with the letter 'Y'. This prefix was used as a holding number for men who had expressed an interest in joining the Royal Navy but who had yet to be called up. Once a man actually joined the service, he was given a service number with the appropriate prefix for his branch.

The records of Royal Navy ratings in the series ADM 188 are available online and you can search the records by name.

## Operational records

A significant percentage of operational records from 1939 onwards are described by the codename under which the operation was planned and executed. There are a number of published and unpublished guides to operational codenames: *Code-names of World War II*

*(1939–1945)* by G. J. Webster, kept behind the desk in the Research Enquiries Room, is a very useful starting point.

### Civilians employed in the armed forces

Unless a civilian employed by the Admiralty, War Office or Air Ministry rose to the higher ranks of the Civil Service, finding anything about them will be very difficult. Senior civil officers of the three military departments are mentioned in the Imperial Calendar and may also be found in the *Navy, Army* and *Air Force Lists*. Other civil servants employed by the War Office may be found in the *War Office List*.

Examination results for various Civil Service jobs, including the three services, can be found in CSC 10.

The case files of certain civil servants employed by numerous departments are in the series CSC 11 and are arranged by name.

Information about civilians who received the 1937 Coronation Medal when employed by the Admiralty can be found in ADM 116/3601 and 3602. These two files give brief details about individuals' careers.

The files of eight very senior civil servants employed by the War Office can be found in WO 335.

## Online searching

Thanks to poor handwriting and flawed transcription, searching for Medal Index Cards (WO 372), Royal Navy ratings' records (ADM 188) and many other digitized records requires certain skills peculiar to the electronic age. Search databases and catalogues using wildcards (*); to overcome the potential pitfalls of adhering rigidly to the spelling of a name, it may be more prudent to shorten it, ending it with an *. Combining terms using 'AND' is also a well-tried technique used by the modern-day researcher. Misspelling of a name in the records is always a possibility, however meticulously the files have been entered into the database.

A good example of how information can vary and how wildcard searches can be very important is the case of Private S. Pettit of the Middlesex Regiment. According to the Medal Index Card for his First World War campaign medals, he is shown as L/15622 Private

Stephen Pettit. The index card for his Military Medal shows 15622 Stephen Pettitt. A search using 15622 and Pettit* will pick up both cards. A search using only Pettit and Middlesex Regiment would not produce the required results.

Errors in transcription can reveal themselves much later. A search of the Medal Index Cards (WO 372) revealed over 500 Acting Station Masters instead of Acting Sergeant Majors, and a number of cards for the Somaliland Camel Corps revealed themselves to be for men of the Somerset Light Infantry!

### *The London Gazette* online

Perhaps one of the most frustrating yet potentially rewarding online resources is *The London Gazette*, which is key to so many resources such as officers' records of service, promotions and appointments and details concerning awards for gallantry and meritorious service.

The strengths and weakness of *The London Gazette* online can only be learned by using it. However, some of the following tips may help:

- Always search by the fullest name of the subject individual first. If that fails, you will end up using surname only.
- For all honours and awards, I do not use dropdown options unless really pushed to do so. Not all of the awards are listed, and using them in combination with dates can complicate matters.
- For awards announced in the Second World War to members of the Army or Royal Air Force, use the personal/service number if you know it. Royal Navy ratings' service numbers appear to be too complicated for the search engine!
- The despatches of most campaigns are published in *The London Gazette*, so if you know the name of the author try searching by it. If the despatch was for a campaign or action in a place with an unusual name, try searching by that.
- Searching *The London Gazette* can reveal much that slips past the nose of many researchers simply because most use the gazette for honours and awards only.

## Using the National Archives' Catalogue

There are a number of techniques that can be used when searching for records on the National Archives' Catalogue. Searching by the name of a person or unit will produce plenty of results, but many of them may be unintelligible unless you use the Catalogue correctly.

Any successful Catalogue search will produce the document description on two overlaid pages. The front page, headed 'Quick Reference', will give you a basic description. If you click on the tab marked 'Full Details' you will get more information about the file, but please note that you may need to scroll down the page to get it!

Searches for Second World War Unit War Diaries in WO 166–76 present a partial dilemma, as search results need to be read very carefully. When searching for an infantry or cavalry unit, the unit name and battalion should produce the required results. Searching for a unit or a corps, for example the Royal Artillery, may be more time-consuming but it is possible to find most diaries if you follow these tips and read carefully.

Searching for 36 Light Anti-Aircraft Regiment,

Royal Artillery, in the United Kingdom in 1942, using the full unit description, for example, will not produce any results. Searching using only '36' produces nine results. If you click on each result in turn, you will find that reading the 'Context Page' carefully reveals how each of the nine results is further described in the hierarchical catalogue. The reference for 36 Light Anti-Aircraft Regiment is WO 166/7634.

Using the Catalogue effectively only comes with frequent use and can be time-consuming until you are happy using it.

### Cases to make you think

The following cases are just four of many that can be used to make you think about using the available information and how to use all available sources.

*Ernest Nash*
My first experience of using the National Archives (or the Public Record Office as it once was) was in 1980. I have been a medal collector for over 30 years and much of what I have learned over the years has been derived from my own research.

In my medal collection for a second time (I sold it once) is an India General Service Medal 1854–95 with the clasp 'Waziristan 1894–5' to 2995 Corporal E. Nash, 2nd Battalion Border Regiment. When I first owned this medal, after checking the medal roll for it in WO 100/75 I sought to locate Nash's record of service in WO 97. I checked both the 1883–1900 and the 1900–13 discharge periods, but without success. I like to have medals with a record of service so that I know something about the recipient. As Nash had no papers, I sold the medal in order to buy something else.

Over 10 years later Nash's medal appeared on the market, and rather than just dismiss it as not having papers I looked a little wider. Since I had first owned the medal, the records of service for men who had seen service in the First World War had been made available in WO 363 and WO 364. I knew Nash's rank, number and unit from 1894–5, so I had another look for his record of service.

It is very important to read the records in WO 363 and WO 364 with great care: what you are looking for on a page may be hidden in a corner or at the side and not blazoned across the top. Eventually I found a record of service for a 3291 Ernest Edwin Nash, 1 Bn Royal Munster Fusiliers, and tucked into the top left-hand corner was 'Border' written over the number 2995. I had found him.

Ernest Edwin Nash was born in Hitchin, Hertfordshire, in 1872 and joined the Army in January 1890 on a short service engagement of seven years with the colours and five years in the reserve. Nash transferred to the Border Regiment in July 1890 and went to India in November 1891. After operational service in Waziristan, and having served his seven years with the colours, Nash transferred to the Army Reserve on 23 November 1897.

Recalled to the colours on 13 November 1899 after the outbreak of the Second Boer/South African War, Nash served with the 3rd Battalion Border Regiment and the 6th Provisional Battalion until finally released from the Army on 16 April 1902.

In October 1914, like many old soldiers, Nash rejoined the Army, this time enlisting in the 20th Battalion, London Regiment. He was promoted from Private to Sergeant on the day of his re-enlistment, and after serving with other battalions of the London Regiment in 1914 and 1915 he transferred into the Royal Defence Corps in April 1916, serving with them until he was finally discharged from the Army for the final time in November 1919.

Ernest Nash died at Lewisham Hospital on 23 May 1940 aged 67, just as the Army was in need of him yet again.

POINTS TO NOTE

- If you are looking for a soldier who served in the Army prior to 1914 and who left between 1883 and 1913 but have not found his record in WO 97, try the First World War papers.
- Ernest Nash was 41 when he volunteered to rejoin the Army in 1914. The maximum age for conscription was 56. Boer War veterans were in most cases young enough to be conscripted if they were not already serving or had not volunteered as Ernest Nash did.
- Read records carefully.

*Arthur Spencer*

During the First World War, personnel who

saw service with the flying services, the Royal Flying Corps, Royal Naval Air Service and Royal Air Force, could have arrived there via a number of different routes. Looking for the record of service of a Royal Flying Corps, Royal Naval Air Service or Royal Air Force person may require more than one search. If the individual was commissioned from the ranks, your search may mean looking at records across a number of different records series of the War Office (WO), the Admiralty (ADM) and the Air Ministry (AIR).

Arthur Spencer joined the Royal Naval Air Service as Petty Officer (Mechanic) on 9 November 1914 and was given the official number F 1769. As a Royal Naval Air Service rating, Spencer's record of service can be found with other Royal Navy ratings' records in ADM 188. All Royal Naval Air Service ratings joining the service after July 1914 were given official numbers prefixed with 'F'. Men from other branches of the Royal Navy who transferred into the Royal Naval Air Service usually kept their original official number but were given Royal Naval Air Service ranks. The records of all naval ratings in ADM 188 have been digitized and are available on DocumentsOnline.

According to Spencer's record of service in ADM 188/563, he was commissioned as Probationary Flight Sub Lieutenant in the Royal Naval Air Service on 5 September 1915. The records of service for Royal Naval Air Service officers can be found in the series ADM 273, and there is a name index for this series which provides volume and page number for each officer. According to the name index, there are three records for Arthur Spencer in ADM 273: in ADM 273/7 ff4, ADM 273/23 ff211 and ADM 273/30 ff133.

After basic flying training at Eastchurch, Arthur Spencer was awarded Royal Aero Club certificate No. 1903 on 16 October 1915. He moved to the Royal Naval Air Service Air Station at Killingholm for further training, but it appears that Spencer's flying career did not last much longer. On 7 November 1915, while he was flying BE2C serial number 1137, the aircraft nose-dived into the Humber. As a result of this accident Spencer lost his flying nerve. According to ADM 273/7, Spencer relinquished his commission in the Royal Naval Air

Service on 24 January 1916. On the same day he was commissioned as a Temporary Sub Lieutenant in the Royal Naval Volunteer Reserve.

The records of service of Royal Naval Volunteer Reserve officers are in the series ADM 337, and once again there is a name index giving volume and page number. Arthur Spencer's Royal Naval Volunteer Reserve record of service is in ADM 337/121 ff66. This record confirms that he was previously in the Royal Naval Air Service and that his new commission was as an armaments officer serving with the Royal Naval Air Service!

After service at Pembroke Air Station in Wales and then at Cattewater in Plymouth, Arthur Spencer's commission in the Royal Naval Volunteer Reserve was terminated on transfer to the Royal Air Force. The final part of his career can be found in the records of service for Royal Air Force officers in AIR 76. AIR 76/477 once again confirms Spencer's previous service in the Royal Naval Volunteer Reserve but adds little more. As he was of no further use to the Royal Air Force, Spencer was transferred to their unemployed list as a

Captain Royal Air Force on 3 February 1919.

POINT TO NOTE
- Be very careful when researching men of the flying services and ensure that you use the *Army, Navy* and *Air Force Lists* if you are looking for an officer.

*The Hook brothers*
During the First World War, many members of the same family served in the armed forces and many of them fought and died together. Duncan and Robin Hook were born in Farnham in Surrey, Duncan on 7 July 1888 and Robin on 12 November 1890. At the outbreak of the First World War they were working as civil engineers in Canada, their father living in Vancouver.

Resigning from their well-paid jobs in Canada, the Hook brothers answered the call of their country of birth and travelled back to England to enlist. On 22 October 1914, they enlisted in the Inns of Court Officer Training Corps, Duncan being given the regimental number 1935 and Robin 1929.

After successfully training to be officers, both Robin and Duncan Hook were commissioned on 15 November 1914 into the 9th (Service) Battalion of the Lancashire Fusiliers; the 9th Lancashire Fusiliers were formed on 31 August 1914 at Bury in Lancashire. After training in Lincolnshire and Surrey, the regiment embarked, as part of 34th Infantry Brigade, 11th (Northern) Division, at Devonport on 5 July 1915 for Egypt. They arrived at Alexandria on 17 July, but their stay in Egypt was short-lived and they were on the island of Imbros by 24 July.

On 6 August 1915, the 9th Lancashire Fusiliers took part in the landings at Suvla Bay, part of the Gallipoli Campaign, arriving at Suvla Bay after 6 pm. The landing was opposed by the Turkish army, with many of the men killed as they tried to wade ashore. Over the next four days, the Hook brothers' regiment saw plenty of vicious fighting, with many officers being killed or wounded. Unfortunately, within these four days the Hook brothers were both killed. Lieutenant Duncan Hook was killed on 7 August and 2nd Lieutenant Robin Hook was killed at some time between 9 and 11 August, but almost certainly 9 August. Although the Unit War Diary of the 9th Lancashire Fusiliers does not record their deaths in detail, the brothers are both listed among the officer casualties.

The records of service of the Hook brothers can be found in WO 339/1610 and 1611. Among the papers are copies of the War Office telegrams sent to their father in Canada, notifying him of their deaths, and two very poignant replies from their father, acknowledging the reports of their deaths.

A report of the deaths of Duncan and Robin Hook was published in the *Calgary Herald*, and a picture of Robin Hook in his uniform was published in *The Illustrated London News* among a collection of portraits of officers who had been killed in action. Duncan and Robin Hook are buried side by side in Hill 10 Cemetery in Gallipoli, not too far from where they were killed.

POINT TO NOTE

• Prior to the release of the records of service, it was an unfortunate fact that it was easier to research someone who died in the First World War than someone who survived! Using the end of a life as the starting point for research can make things simpler: you just go backwards.

*The Unknown Englishman*

People (especially agents) who served with the Special Operations Executive in many cases used more than one name. The real name of an individual and their alias(es) and codenames can get mixed up, and unless careful attention is paid to the records, their content and how they may be described on the Catalogue, it is possible to use the wrong name(s) when pursuing your research.

Gabor Adler was born in Satumare, Hungary, in 1919 and was of Jewish descent. After various jobs, including being a waiter in Algiers, he eventually found himself in Gibraltar.

After serving in the Auxiliary Military Pioneer Corps as a Private, Adler was recruited by the Special Operations Executive in February 1942. He was given the name John Armstrong and was commissioned as a Lieutenant on the *General List*. According to his record of service, Adler's commission was not announced in *The London Gazette* but was on a secret list. Adler was also known as Guiseppe Bianci and Gabriele Bianci, both of which names are only recorded on his record of service. The possession of so many aliases was quite normal for Special Operations Executive agents.

After his training 'John Armstrong' was sent on operations. He was landed from a submarine near Cagliari, Sardinia, in early January 1943 as part of Operation Moselle, and seems to have been captured within 24 hours by Italian coastguards. Armstrong's story after his capture is very vague but he was known to be in Rome, in the hands of the Italian authorities as a prisoner in Regina Coeli Prison. After the Italians capitulated, Adler was eventually passed into German hands in about October 1943. Although his exact date of death is not known, it appears that Adler was killed just before the liberation of Rome.

In the Army Roll of Honour in WO 304 there is no entry for Armstrong but there is one for Adler. There is also an entry for Adler on the Commonwealth War Graves Commission 'Debt of Honour' register, noting that he died on 1 June 1944 and that he is commemorated on the Cassino Memorial. But it does not record a grave.

Gabor Adler is buried in a grave in Rome currently marked 'The Unknown Englishman'.

Hopefully it will eventually be marked with the correct personal information. Gabor Adler's Special Operations Executive file can be found in HS 9/9/3.

POINTS TO NOTE
- Aliases create false trails, so tread carefully.
- The HS 9 catalogue will in many cases note the real name of the Special Operations Executive agent and sometimes their alias(es) or AKA (Also Known As).

## QUICK REFERENCES

### Records of service

| *Army* | OFFICERS | OTHER RANKS |
|---|---|---|
| Pre-First World War | WO 25 | WO 97 |
| | WO 76 | PIN 71 |
| | | |
| First World War | WO 339 | WO 363 |
| | WO 374 | WO 364 |
| | PIN 26 | PIN 26 |
| | | |
| *Militia* | WO 68 | WO 96 |
| *Imperial Yeomanry* | – | WO 128 |
| | – | WO 129 |
| *Royal Garrison Regiment* | WO 19 | WO 96 |
| *South African Local Forces* | – | WO 126 |
| | – | WO 127 |

| *Royal Navy* | OFFICERS | RATINGS |
|---|---|---|
| | ADM 196 | ADM 188 |
| | ADM 340 | – |
| *Royal Naval Reserve* | ADM 240 | BT 164 |
| | ADM 340 | BT 377 |
| *Royal Naval Volunteer Reserve* | ADM 337 | ADM 337 |
| *Royal Naval Division* | ADM 339 | ADM 339 |
| | | |
| *Royal Marines* | ADM 196 | ADM 157 |
| | – | ADM 159 |
| *Royal Naval Air Service* | ADM 273 | ADM 188 |
| *Women's Royal Naval Service* | ADM 318 | ADM 336 |
| *Royal Flying Corps* | WO 339 | WO 363 |
| | WO 374 | WO 364 |
| *Royal Air Force* | AIR 76 | AIR 79 |
| *Women's Royal Air Force* | – | AIR 80 |
| *Special Operations Executive* | HS 9 | |
| *Women's Land Army* | MAF 421 | |

## Operations (key series)

| **Pre-1914** | **1914–18** | **1919–39** | **1939–45** | **1946–53** |
|---|---|---|---|---|
| ARMY | | | | |
| WO 32, WO 105 | WO 95 | WO 32 | WO 166–77 | WO 261–71 |
| WO 33, | WO 158 | WO 191 | WO 275 | WO 108 |
| | | | | WO 281 |
| | | | | WO 308 |
| | | | | |
| ROYAL NAVY | | | | |
| ADM 1 | ADM 1 | ADM 1 | ADM 1 | ADM 1 |
| ADM 53 | ADM 53 | ADM 53 | ADM 53 | ADM 53 |

| Pre-1914 | 1914–18 | 1919–39 | 1939–45 | 1946–53 |
|---|---|---|---|---|
| ADM 116 | ADM 116 | ADM 116 | ADM 116 | ADM 116 |
|  | ADM 137 | ADM 137 |  |  |
|  | ADM 173 | ADM 173 | ADM 173 | ADM 173 |
|  |  |  | ADM 199 |  |

ROYAL MARINES (ONLY)

|  |  |  | ADM 202 | ADM 202 |
|---|---|---|---|---|

ROYAL AIR FORCE

|  | AIR 1 | AIR 5 |  |  |
|---|---|---|---|---|
|  |  | AIR 8 |  |  |
|  |  | AIR 23 |  |  |
|  |  | AIR 27 | AIR 27 | AIR 27 |

SPECIAL OPERATIONS EXECUTIVE

|  |  |  | HS 1–6 |  |
|---|---|---|---|---|

## Army order of precedence

The following order of precedence is applicable to the First World War period but it does represent information that may be needed to use many of the records for the 1900–20 period. The order is based on the date specific units were originally founded. The number at the end of each infantry regiment, starting with the Royal Scots, is the original numerical identity of the unit prior to 1881 and is the number used to identify the regiment in the index of officers' Long Numbers in WO 338.

ARMY ORDER OF PRECEDENCE
1 Life Guards
2 Life Guards
Royal Horse Guards
Household Battalion
Royal Horse Artillery
1 King's Dragoon Guards
2 Dragoon Guards (Queen's Bays)
3 (Prince of Wales's) Dragoon Guards
4 (Royal Irish) Dragoon Guards
5 (Princess Charlotte of Wales's) Dragoon Guards
6 Dragoon Guards (Carabiniers)
7 (The Princess Royal's) Dragoon Guards
1 (Royal) Dragoons
2 Dragoons (Royal Scots Greys)
3 (King's Own) Hussars
4 (The Queen's Own) Hussars
5 (Royal Irish) Lancers
6 (Inniskilling) Dragoons
7 (Queen's Own) Hussars
8 The King's (Royal Irish) Hussars
9 (Queen's Royal) Lancers
10 (The Prince of Wales's Own) Hussars
11 (Prince Albert's Own) Hussars
12 (The Prince of Wales's Royal) Lancers
13 Hussars
14 (King's) Hussars
15 (King's) Hussars
16 (The Queen's) Lancers
17 Lancers (Duke of Cambridge's Own)
18 Hussars
19 Hussars
20 Hussars
21 (Empress of India's) Lancers

The Yeomanry Regiments
Royal Artillery
Royal Field Artillery
Royal Engineers
Royal Flying Corps
Grenadier Guards
Coldstream Guards
Scots Guards
Irish Guards
Welsh Guards
Royal Scots (Lothian) 1
Queen's (Royal West Surrey) 2
Buffs (East Kent) 3
King's Own (Royal Lancaster) 4
Northumberland Fusiliers 5
Royal Warwickshire 6
Royal Fusiliers (City of London) 7
The King's (Liverpool) 8
Norfolk 9
Lincolnshire 10
Devonshire 11
Suffolk 12
Prince Albert's (Somerset Light Infantry) 13
Prince of Wales's Own (East Yorkshire) 14
East Yorkshire 15
Bedfordshire 16
Leicestershire 17
Royal Irish 18
Alexandra, Princess of Wales's (Yorkshire) 19
Lancashire Fusiliers 20
Royal Scots Fusiliers 21
Cheshire 22
Royal Welsh Fusiliers 23

South Wales Borderers **24**
King's Own Scottish Borderers **25**
Cameronians (Scottish Rifles) **26**
Royal Inniskilling Fusiliers **27**
Gloucestershire **28**
Worcestershire **29**
East Lancashire **30**
East Surrey **31**
Duke of Cornwall's Light Infantry **32**
Duke of Wellington's (West Riding) **33**
Border **34**
Royal Sussex **35**
Hampshire **37**
South Staffordshire **38**
Dorsetshire **39**
Prince of Wales's Volunteers (South Lancashire) **40**
Welsh **41**
Black Watch (Royal Highlanders) **42**
Oxfordshire and Buckinghamshire Light Infantry **43**
Essex **44**
Sherwood Foresters (Nottinghamshire and Derbyshire) **45**
Loyal North Lancashire **47**
Northamptonshire **48**
Princess Charlotte of Wales's (Royal Berkshire) **49**
Queen's Own (Royal West Kent) **50**
King's Own (Yorkshire Light Infantry) **51**
King's (Shropshire Light Infantry) **53**
Duke of Cambridge's Own (Middlesex) **57**
King's Royal Rifle Corps **60**
Duke of Edinburgh's (Wiltshire) **62**
Manchester **63**
Prince of Wales's (North Staffordshire) **64**
York and Lancaster **65**

Durham Light Infantry **68**
Highland Light Infantry **71**
Seaforth Highlanders (Ross-shire Buffs, The Duke of
Albany's) **72**
Gordon Highlanders **75**
Queen's Own Cameron Highlanders **79**
Royal Irish Rifles **83**
Princess Victoria's (Royal Irish Fusiliers) **87**
Connaught Rangers **88**
Princess Louise's (Argyll and Sutherland Highlanders) **91**
Prince of Wales's Leinster (Royal Canadians) **100**
Royal Munster Fusiliers **101**
Royal Dublin Fusiliers **102**
Rifle Brigade
Royal Army Chaplains Department
Army Service Corps
Royal Army Medical Corps
Army Ordnance Corps
Army Veterinary Corps
Machine Gun Corps
Royal Tank Corps
Labour Corps
Honourable Artillery Company
Monmouthshire Regiment
Cambridgeshire Regiment
London Regiment
Hertfordshire Regiment
Northern Cyclist Battalion
Highland Cyclist Battalion
Kent Cyclist Battalion
Huntingdon Cyclist Battalion.

This order of precedence is based on the *Army*

*List* of August 1914, to which have been added a number of units created between 1914 and 1918.

A number of Irish regiments were disbanded in 1922 and other units, such as the Parachute Regiment and the Special Air Service, were created in the Second World War. In order to see more recent orders of precedence, use the *Army List*.

### Ranks

*Officers*

The following lists show the most common officer ranks. Individuals such as surgeons, paymasters and chaplains also had officer status.

| ROYAL NAVY | ARMY | ROYAL AIR FORCE |
|---|---|---|
| Admiral of the Fleet | Field Marshal | Marshal of the Royal Air Force |
| Admiral | General | Air Chief Marshal |
| Vice Admiral | Lieutenant General | Air Marshal |
| Rear Admiral | Major General | Air Vice Marshal |
| Commodore | Brigadier | Air Commodore |
| Captain | Colonel | Group Captain |
| Commander | Lieutenant Colonel | Wing Commander |
| Lieutenant Commander | Major | Squadron Leader |
| Lieutenant | Captain | Flight Lieutenant |
| Sub Lieutenant | Lieutenant | Flying Officer |
| Midshipman | Second Lieutenant | Pilot Officer |

## Other ranks

Over the period this book covers, the titles of other ranks of all three services have changed on numerous occasions. In the Army many titles used at the lowest rank vary according to regiment or corps. Some ranks are unique to specific parts of the Army. The following is just a basic list of ranks and their equivalents (not necessarily equal in status) in each service. The Royal Marines used similar ranks to the Army.

## Warrant Officers

| ROYAL NAVY | ARMY | ROYAL AIR FORCE |
|---|---|---|
| Boatswain | Regimental Sergeant Major | Warrant Officer |
| Gunner | Conductor | Sergeant Major 1 |
| Carpenter | Master Gunner 1 | |
| Shipwright | Schoolmaster | |
| Cooper | Bandmaster | |
| | Company Quartermaster Sergeant | Sergeant Major 2 |
| | Troop Sergeant Major | |
| | Company Sergeant Major | |

### *Senior non-commissioned officers*

| ROYAL NAVY | ARMY | ROYAL AIR FORCE |
|---|---|---|
| Chief Petty Officer | Staff Sergeant | Flight Sergeant |
| Petty Officer | Sergeant | Sergeant |

### *Junior non-commissioned officers*

| ROYAL NAVY | ARMY | ROYAL AIR FORCE |
|---|---|---|
| Leading Rate | Corporal | Corporal |

### *Men*

| ROYAL NAVY | ARMY | ROYAL AIR FORCE |
|---|---|---|
| Able Rate | Lance Corporal | Senior Aircraftsman |
| Ordinary Rate | Private | Leading Aircraftsman |

In the Army, ranks such as Gunner, Trooper, Pioneer, Sapper or Rifleman are all equivalent to Private.

# Useful addresses and websites

## ADDRESSES

### General

**British Empire & Commonwealth Museum**, Clock Tower Yard, Temple Meads, Bristol BS1 6QH, Tel: 0117 925 4980, *www.empiremuseum.co.uk*

**British Library**, 96 Euston Road, London NW1 2DB, Tel: 020 7412 7332, *www.bl.uk*

**British Library Newspaper Collection**, Colindale Avenue, London NW9 5HE, Tel: 020 7412 7353, *www.bl.uk/collections/newspapers.html*

**Commonwealth War Graves Commission**, 2 Marlow Road, Maidenhead, Berkshire SL6 7DX, *www.cwgc.org*

**Home Office Immigration and Nationality Directorate**, Reliance House, 20 Water Street, Liverpool L2 8XU, *www.ind.homeoffice.gov.uk*

**Imperial War Museum London**, Lambeth Road, London SE1 6HZ, Tel: 020 7416 5320/5321, *www.iwm.org.uk*

**Ministry of Defence Army Personnel Centre**, Historical Disclosures, Mailpoint 400, Kentigen House, 65 Brown Street, Glasgow G2 8EX, Tel: 0141 224 3515 *www.mod.uk/contacts/army_records.htm*

**The National Archives**, Kew, Richmond, Surrey TW9 4DU, Tel: 020 8876 3444, *www.nationalarchives.gov.uk*

**National Archives of Scotland**, HM General Register House, Edinburgh, EH1 3YY, Tel: 0131 535 1314 *www.nas.gov.uk*

**National Army Museum**, Royal Hospital Road, Chelsea, London SW3 4HT, Tel: 020 7730 0717, *www.national-army-museum.ac.uk*

**National Library of Wales**, Aberystwyth, Ceredigion, Wales SY23 3BU, Tel: 01970 632800

**National Maritime Museum**, Maritime Information Centre, Romney Road, London SE10 9NF, Tel: 020 8858 4422, *www.nmm.ac.uk*

**Navy Search**, TNT Archive Services, Tetron Point, William Nadin Way, Swadlincote, Derbyshire DE11 0BB, Tel: 01283 227912, *www.mod.uk/contacts/rn_records.htm*

**Office for National Statistics**, Certificate Enquiries, PO Box 2, Southport, Merseyside PR8 2JD, Tel: 01283 227912, *www.gro.gov.uk/gro/content/certificates/*

**Principal Probate Registry**, Probate Department, Principal Registry of the Family Division, First Avenue House, 42–49 High Holborn, London WC1V 6NP, Tel: 020 7047 6939/6946/6043/7431/7414

**Royal Air Force**, PMA Sec IM1B, Room 5, Building 248A, RAF Personnel Management Agency, RAF Innsworth, Gloucester GL3 1EZ

**Society of Genealogists**, 14 Charterhouse Buildings, Goswell Road, London EN1M 7BA, Tel: 020 7251 8799, *www.sog.org.uk*

### Ministry of Defence addresses

The addresses are for post-First World War records of service.

THE ARMY
Army Personnel Centre, Historical Disclosures, Mail Point 400, Kentigern House, 65 Brown Street, Glasgow, G2 8EX

THE ROYAL NAVY AND ROYAL MARINES
DNCM, Data Protection Cell, Building 1/152,
   PP65 Victory View HMNB Portsmouth
   PO1 3LS, Tel: 02392 727531/723114/726063

THE ROYAL AIR FORCE
PMA 1M 1B RAF, Room 5, Building 248A,
   RAF Personnel Management Agency, RAF
   Innsworth, Gloucester GL3 1EZ,
   Tel: 01452 712612, ext. 7622

HOME GUARD RECORDS OF SERVICE
TNT Archive Service, Tetron Point, William
   Nadin Way, Swadlincote, Derbyshire
   DE11 0BB, Tel: 01283 227 911/912/913,
   Fax: 01283 227 942

## WEBSITES

*www.a2a.org.uk* The Access to Archives
   database
*www.ancestry.co.uk* Access to records
   digitized by Ancestry. Downloads are by
   payment
*www.archives.ca* Library and Archives Canada
*www.awm.gov.au* The Australian War
   Memorial. Access to digitized records
   concering the Australian Forces

*<http://archives.govt.nz/>* Archives New
   Zealand
*www.britishorigins.com* Pay-per-view site
   offering access to a wide range of records
*www.collectionscanada.ca/archivianet/020118
   02_e.html* For migrants to Canada between
   1926 and 1935
*www.fco.gov.uk/travel* The Foreign and
   Commonwealth Office
*<http://freepages.genealogy.rootsweb.com/-
   britishhomechildren>* Essential site for
   researching the British Home children who
   were sent to Canada between 1870 and
   1940
*www.gazettes-online.co.uk* *The London
   Gazette* online, used for honours and
   awards
*www.gitrace.org* Helpful advice and sources
   used to trace US GI fathers
*www.naa.gov.au* National Archives of Australia
*www.nationalarchives.gov.uk/nra/* The
   National Register of Archives
*www.nationalarchives.gov.uk/catalogue* The
   National Archives online catalogue
*www.nationalarchives.gov.uk/documentsonline*
   The National Archives documents online

*www.national.archives.gov.za*  National Archives of South Africa

*www.1914-1918.net*  Information portal for advice about the First World War

*www.rootsweb.com*  Includes names of passengers from a multitude of ports from 1500s to 1900s

*www.scotlandspeople.gov.uk*  Access to births, marriages and deaths indexes, census returns and parish registers for Scotland

*www.veterans-uk.info/index.html*  Pages of the MOD hosted Veteran's Agency

# Further reading

A. Adolph, *Tracing your Family History*
(Collins, 2004)

D. Annal, *Easy Family History* (The National
Archives, 2005)

Kevin Asplin, *The Roll of the Imperial
Yeomanry, Scottish Horse and Lovats
Scouts: 2nd Boor War, 1899 1902*
(Salisbury, 2000)

Amanda Bevan, *Tracing Your Ancestors in the
National Archives*, 7th edition (The National
Archives, 2006)

Peter Christian, *The Genealogist's Internet*,
3rd edition (The National Archives, 2005)

J. Cole and J. Titford, *Tracing your Family Tree*
(Countryside Books, 2004)

J.J. Colledge, *Ships of the Royal Navy*
(Greenhill, 2003)

S. Colwell, *The National Archives: a practical
guide for family historians* (The National
Archives, 2006)

K.J. Douglas-Morris, *Naval Long Service Medals 1830–1990* (Privately published, 1991)

T. Henshaw, *The Sky Their Battlefield* (Grub Street, 1995)

M. Herber, *AncestralTrails* (Sutton, 2004)

D. Hey, *Journeys in Family History* (The National Archives, 2004)

*Honours and Awards: Army, Navy and Air Force 1914–20* (Hayward, 1974)

R. Kershaw and M. Pearsall, *Family History on the Move* (The National Archives, 2006)

*Military Museums in the UK* (2006 Army Museums Ogilby Trust)

Bruno Pappalardo, *Tracing Your Naval Ancestors* (Public Record Office, 2003)

M. Pearsall, *Family History Companion* (The National Archives, 2007)

C. Shores, N. Franks and R. Guest, *Above the Trenches* (Grub Street, 1990)

K. Smith, C.T. Watts and M.J. Watts, *Records of Merchant Shipping and Seamen* (Public Record Office, 1998)

William Spencer, *Air Force Records: A Guide for Family Historians* (The National Archives, 2008)

William Spencer, *Army Service Records: A Guide for Family Historians* (The National Archives, 2008)

William Spencer, *First World War Army Service Records* (The National Archives, 2008)

William Spencer, *Medals: The Researcher's Guide* (The National Archives, 2006)

Geoff Swinfield, *Smart Family History* (The National Archives, 2006)

*War Office and Associated Records List and Index LIII* (List and Index Society, 1962)

Ben Warlow, *Shore Establishments of the Royal Navy* (Maritime Books, 1992)

C.T. Watts and M.J. Watts, *My Ancestor Was a Merchant Seaman* (Federation of Family History Societies, 2002)

## Picture captions and credits

Front cover:  Soldiers leaving on a train, First World War. (Photograph Q_27724, courtesy of the Imperial War Museum, London.)

Back cover:  American servicemen and women gather in Paris to celebrate the surrender of the Japanese, 15 August 1945. (Getty Images)

p. vi  British troops, Battle of Scarpe, April 1917. (Photograph Q_006228 by courtesy of the Imperial War Museum, London.)

p. 6  The *Navy List* for June 1941 showing the officers of HMS *Hood*. (TNA ADM 177/34)

p. 14  135th Seige Battery artificers attending to their Howitzers at La Houssaye, August 1916. (Photograph Q_004147 by courtesy of the Imperial War Museum, London.)

p. 24  A telegram from the War Office informing Duncan Hook's father that he was killed in action. (TNA WO 339/1610)

p. 36  A letter from Duncan Hook's father acknowledging the War Office's telegram informing him of his son's death. (TNA WO 339/1610)

p. 70  Royal Navy Auxiliary Service record of service from November 1914 for Arthur Bedward Spencer. (TNA ADM 188/563)

p. 116  The *Air Force List* April-June 1933. (TNA)

p. 134  The *Home Guard List* 1944 showing the officers of the 2nd Huntingdonshire Battalion. (TNA)

p. 148  The *Army List* for July 1942 showing officers of the South Wales Borderers. (TNA)

p.164  Sergeant Charles Trevor Keeling of the Royal Air Force was a prisoner of war. On his return he had to fill in this repatriation questionnaire. (TNA WO 344/170/1)

p. 172  The crew with their Avro Lancaster. Use of the Lancaster continued for a number of years after the Second World War. (TNA INF 2/42)

p. 178  The log book of HMS *Duke of York* 26 December 1943 recording the sinking of Scharnhorst. (TNA ADM 53/117405)

p. 184  A Home Office Aliens Registration card for Marie Eisner, July 1940. (TNA HO 396/18 f609/610)

p. 194  The King's Own Scottish Borderers' war diary while serving in Korea, November 1951. (TNA WO 281/485)

# Index